MY FIVE STONES –
A MEMOIR

By Susan Darin Pohl

ISBN: 0615724280
ISBN-13: 9780615724287

Library of Congress Control Number: 2012921222
Susan Darin Pohl
Oakland, CA

AUTHOR'S NOTE

This book is a memoir, drawn from my own experiences and memories. All of the names of the people who worked and lived in the prison have been changed to afford them privacy. Although all of the incidents are true to the best of my recollection, some of the people presented are composite characters drawn from more than one person's experience.

DEDICATION

I dedicate this book to all of the women in the world who are now, or who have ever been, imprisoned physically, mentally, or spiritually. May you be free from suffering, may you be free from loneliness, may you be free from fear, and may you be free from despair. May you find the guiding source of your inner strength and live the life you were meant to live.

PROLOGUE

Once upon a time there was a beautiful gray sea gull. The sea gull loved to spread its wings and fly high over the ocean where it fished. One day, it had soared higher and farther than it had ever gone before. It played with the drafts of wind as it swooped in and out of the air currents and down toward the water of the ocean. The sea gull was having so much fun that it did not notice the dark and angry storm clouds that were gathering on the horizon. The sea gull only wanted to play and catch fish, and so she was unaware of the storm brewing around her.

Suddenly, as if out of nowhere, a huge wind smacked the sea gull in the face and got her attention. Now the sea gull was alarmed. She started crying and trying to fly back to the safety of the shore. The harder she flapped her wings the more exhausted she became. She realized that she was making no progress against the storm, but she could not help herself. With every gust of wind, she flew directly into the storm only thinking of the safety on shore.

In the distance, far out on the horizon, an old wise sea gull sat on a buoy waiting for the storm to pass. She watched as the young sea gull fought the storm and became more and more exhausted. She needs to change directions the old sea gull thought. She needs to fly away from what she sees as safety. The old sea gull began to call and screech wildly to the young one hoping her voice would carry above the storm.

TABLE OF CONTENTS

Chapter One

INSIDE PRISON WALLS

It is said that no one truly knows a nation until one has been inside its jails. A nation should not be judged by how it treats its highest citizens but it lowest ones. —Nelson Mandela

The rectangular room was empty and locked. Looking through the windows it appeared cold, white, and antiseptic. A guard in uniform eventually came and slowly unlocked the double doors and held them open for us to pass through. Several long rectangular tables were pushed against the wall in the back of the room. They were covered with plain white paper table cloths and an arrangement of paper cups filled with red and green punch. There were also cookies neatly stacked and unopened in their cellophane packages. People were congregating in the back, nervously picking up their cups and trying to open the sealed cookies. I decided finding a seat was more important than cookies, a first for me, and so I chose a table near the back of the room. I put my seminary bag under the table and sat on the cold metal chair. The tables in the back quickly filled up while the tables that were located in the front of the room, like pews in the front of a church, remained empty. A young man approached the front of the room and we turned toward him as he began to speak.

"All right people. Listen up. Lesson number one: the primary concern of the prison is the safety and security of the inmates. Whatever your particular program, and no matter how important you think it is, it's secondary to security. You got that? What does this mean to you? Well, it means that some days you come out here, and you can't get in because there's something going on in the compound. It may be because we have fog that has come in; it may be because we have a special inspection going on. The thing you need to know is that we decide if volunteers can enter or not. Our goals are safety and security, not the implementation of your programs."

He was tall, with closely cropped blond hair, and a muscular build; he could have been someone sent over by the Actor's Studio to play the part of a Nazi guard. His posture conveyed to us that he was not someone to mess with. As new volunteers at a federal prison, he was our first encounter with a member of the prison staff. He sat casually on the edge of the desk, his legs apart, with one foot on the floor, the other dangling in the air.

"Lesson two: if people are on the compound running, you start running too. In the same direction everyone else is running. No one runs unless there's a problem. Get it? Never run on the compound unless it is an emergency."

"Lesson number three: the inmates are always to be referred to by their last name, and the same goes for you. You are never to share any personal information with them about your life. The point of this should be obvious to you."

"Lesson number four: inmates are not allowed to have contraband. What is contraband? Anything that is not issued by the BOP, that's the Bureau of Prisons to you."

"What about prayer cards?" one of the new chaplains asks. The woman across from me and I glance at each other, and she does a very slight eye roll.

"Do you have twelve hundred cards to give to each inmate? No? Then it is considered contraband. Next question?"

"What about pencils? What if they come to class and don't have a pencil?" one of the teachers asks.

"Send them out and tell them to bring a pencil next time. Any other questions? Ok," he continued, slowly standing up, and pacing in the front of the room. "Suppose someone asks you for a stamp? They say it's their mother's birthday. Could you please bring in a stamp for them next time? It is such a little thing. What's the answer?"

The audience murmurs, "No."

"The answer is no. Why is the answer no?"

Silence meets this question. It did seem a little mean not to give an inmate a stamp for her mother's birthday card.

"The reason is twofold: one, if it isn't Bureau of Prison issued, what is it considered?"

"Contraband," we all answered correctly.

"The second reason is one of boundaries. First it's a stamp, and then what will they want next? The answer is always 'No.' Let me tell you a little story. One of our staff people keeps a bowl of Skittles on her desk. One of the inmates walked up and said gosh, I haven't tasted a Skittle in ages. Could I have one? Now what's the answer here?" A short pause, and we all murmur, "No."

"No? Exactly. It's a slippery slope, first a Skittle or a stamp and then they own you." He glared at all of us and then asked, "How many people here are from the Religious Services Department? Raise your hands." We cautiously put our hands in the air, as the rest of the room turned around to look at us.

"Okay, religious services people. Lesson number five is directly aimed at you. There's no hugging of inmates in the prison. No personal contact. Got that? If an inmate learns that one of her family members has suddenly passed on, you may be tempted to give her a hug, right?" As we shrugged our answer, he glowered at us and said, "No! Here, let me show you how you offer condolences in prison." He asked one of the women near the front to stand up.

"You shake her hand with one hand and pat her shoulder with the other," he said as he demonstrated this rather awkward movement.

"Do you have that, religious services people?" we nodded in unison.

"A handshake is acceptable but no body contact. No hugs. I don't want to hear that any of you volunteers are hugging inmates or you will be out of here in a flash. This is for your protection as well as theirs. If you hug them, they could claim that you were trying to sexually molest them." We all gasped.

"All right next thing. I want to talk to you about something a little unpleasant, and that is the taking of hostages."

At this comment the bookmobile volunteers, turned to each other and started to mutter.

"The BOP has never had a hostage situation. Do you know why?" Clearly we didn't.

"The reason is we don't allow it. Here's how it goes. Say one of the inmates has gotten a weapon, and is holding it at one of your throats. The inmate says let me out or I will kill the hostage. Do you know what our answer is?" He stood and glared at all of us, as we put our heads down, afraid to hear his answer.

"The answer is 'go ahead and kill the hostage, because the bullet that comes out of my gun will certainly kill you'."

A dead silence enveloped the room. Kill the hostage? Hadn't this guy ever heard of peaceful negotiations, a class in nonviolent communications perhaps? But he was on a roll, clearly relishing the sense of horror on our faces.

"Okay. Say you were taken hostage, and neither you nor the inmate has been killed" he paused. I definitely liked this scenario better.

"We break in and tell you to lie on the floor in a fetal position. Instead you decide to get up and say, wait I'm a bookmobile volunteer. We will probably shoot you. Do you know why?" Because you're a jerk, I wondered?

"How do we know that you aren't an inmate who has changed clothes with one of you volunteers? If you are in a hostage situation, you are to do exactly what the officers tell you to do. Do not get up and identity yourself until you are told to do so by an officer. Next, I want to talk about weapons. I've seen inmates who have carved ordinary soap into a cutting weapon that killed someone. I've seen another person who took one of those heating coils for tea, rewired it and electrocuted someone. You cannot overestimate the manipulation and duplicity of these people." He paused, pleased with the dampened enthusiasm in the room. A valiant bookmobile volunteer raised his hand.

"How often have those types of weapons been found here?" he asked with a firm voice that belied his years.

"What? Here?" the guard scoffed at the question.

"Yes," the bookmobile man pressed on. "Here at this prison for women. How many weapons have there been?

"At this women's institution? None. The biggest issue we have here are the hugs, and fights over girlfriends, so religious services people pay attention. The final thing I want to tell you is if you are in an emergency, get to the phone and dial the deuces. That's 2222. You dial that and we will all come running, in the same direction! Good luck and remember the rules."

He slid off the table and swaggered out of the room. There was a definite feeling of deflation in the room after his presentation. We checked out the next presenter, a mild mannered, middle-aged white woman.

"I want to welcome all of you volunteers to this orientation," she began in a more conciliatory tone than our previous presenter. "We refer to this place as the institution, not a prison. Just for clarity, it is a Federal Correctional Institution. In order to come to a federal institution you must have broken a federal law, not a state law. In this institution, fifty-three percent of the women are Hispanic and sixty-one percent are non-citizens. The average age of an inmate here is thirty-six years old and the average sentence is fifty-seven months. We have some women in here for life, and others who have much shorter sentences. Because this is a federal prison, the women here are not eligible for parole. Sixty-five percent of the women are in for drug related offenses, eleven percent for immigration violation, and six percent for robbery. Only two percent of the women who are here have committed violent crimes."

I decided that the statistics did not seem that scary, so I settled in and continued to listen to her.

"FCI Dublin, this facility was opened in 1974. At that time there were 250 people here. By 1977 there were one thousand female inmates. In 1990 they opened up the prison camp across the street. It is a minimum-security level facility and it has three hundred inmates. There are three other federal female facilities: Danbury, Connecticut; Tallahassee, Florida; and Carswell, Texas. We have three hundred volunteers at this facility and we could not operate the institution without you. We very much appreciate you volunteering your time and energy. If you have any questions at all about your time here, please do not hesitate to contact my office."

The woman who had been sitting across from me during the orientation had also raised her hand to indicate that she was from Religious Services. As the orientation ended she smiled at me and we walked out of the room together. We made an instant connection and chatted on our way out to our cars. I found out that her name was Lori and she was a former reporter for the San Jose Mercury News. She had been attending the Lutheran seminary for a long time, taking only a few courses at a time so she could be at home with her kids. We agreed to stick together at the institution.

Several weeks later, I was inching my lime green Volkswagen bug toward the prison checkpoint, following the steady line of cars in front of me. It was September 17, 2001, and security was on high alert at all federal buildings, including this institution. The prison had recently installed concrete protective barriers on the access road that led up to the entrance. The barriers were designed to slow down and manage traffic into the institution. There was no way any vehicle was going to speed past the guards and car bomb this facility. I had originally been scheduled to start this assignment on September 11, 2001. Needless to say my start had been delayed. As the car idled, I tried to manage my fears.

When I reached the checkpoint, I was instructed to exit my vehicle, walk in front of it and stand on the other side of the guard station. One guard used a mirror attached to a long pole and searched under my car. Another guard did a thorough inside search of my VW bug even lifting my yellow Shasta daisy from its plastic vase on the dashboard, to determine that it was, in fact, a fake flower. The guards were tense, and carried machine guns that were pointed at the ground. I felt their wariness roll over me, as I checked out their young, grim faces. Fear, my age-old companion, was riding high in my stomach. I passed the inspection, got back in the car and drove slowly through the military facility and back toward the prison. I was almost there.

Once I had parked the car, I took a deep breath and sorted through my belongings that I kept in my seminary bag. I removed my driver's license from my wallet, and, as instructed, I locked my wallet and purse in the glove compartment. As I stepped outside the car, I noticed my hands were steady, but I could see the thin blue lines of my veins through my skin, and realized my hands were ice cold. I walked briskly toward the glass A-framed building located in the front of the prison walls. It could have been the entrance to any federal park building, except for the high walls that surrounded it, and the concertina wire on top of the walls. As I stood there for a minute in the bright California sun, a flock of geese flew out of the prison and into the nearby hills.

I approached the front desk to introduce myself to the female guard who "processed in" all visitors to the facility. I felt ill at ease and uncertain of the protocol as I approached her desk. The lobby had an antiseptic smell, and stark, white walls with neatly hung photographs of prison personnel. I tried to establish eye contact with the guard and smile at her, but her seat and desk were below the counter. I didn't think she saw me, so I walked up to the counter, and put my elbows on it and leaned toward her to get her attention.

"Hi, I'm the new chaplain intern working with Chaplain Becker." The guard watched me with flat eyes.

"Back up," she said turning off her computer screen. I backed up and smiled at her. She didn't smile back.

"Let me see your driver's license." I reached into my canvas bag, and after some initial fumbling to locate it, I handed it over.

"Chaplain Becker has requested that you get a blue badge, which means you do not need to be escorted on the prison grounds. Do you understand that?"

"Yes ma'am." I said.

"Hand me your bag please," she said reaching for my seminary tote bag. She carefully took everything out, inspected it, and then just as carefully replaced it all. She motioned me toward the metal detection machine.

"Like at the airport," I said trying to establish some connection. No response. I passed through the metal detector one way and then she directed me to turn around and go back through again just the way I came, as a double check. Luckily, I did not set off alarms on either trip. I had previously been warned to avoid underwire bras. I turned to her, waiting to see what I should do next.

"Here," she said holding my bag out for me. I took the bag and stood waiting in front of a white, painted, metal door that had a small rectangular window at the very top.

"Coming through," she hollered into the air. The door in front of me suddenly made a loud clank, and came slightly ajar. I stood there for a moment, and then pulled the heavy metal door toward me. I walked into a narrow rectangular space, and heard a sickening "bam" as the heavy door slammed shut behind me. I was now alone in the sally port between the outside world and the inside prison. I stood still, knowing that I was being watched. A two-way glass covered one side of the wall. I stood there with my seminary bag over my shoulder, wondering why was I here? What had I been thinking?

Serving in a prison was not something I felt called to do. I had nothing in common with these women, and I'm sure they wouldn't want anything to do with an upper-middle-class white woman like me. How could I accomplish anything in an environment that was so repressive and hostile? Why didn't I just stay in Palo Alto where I belonged, working in high tech and making a very good living? The whole idea of going to seminary now seemed stupid and my decision to come out here for a few months seemed really stupid. Now I was stuck in a sally port at a federal prison. What would happen if the guard went for a coffee break and I got left here? How long did it take for them to check me out? Time slowly ticked by. Should I move toward the next door, or stay still? I shifted my weight back and forth, rocking to calm myself. I took a deep breath. I hate this. I hate this.

Bam! The door in front of me made the sound of gunfire as it came unlocked, and I pushed it open, relieved to walk through and into the open air. Later, no matter how many times I went through the sally port, I had similar feelings of anxiety about being left in there, and relief to see the inside of the prison once the door was unlocked. Everything in the prison was designed to be intimidating, from the sounds of the door slamming closed as you entered the prison, to the military titles and formal language used by the guards. In prison it is all about controlling the environment and the peoplAs I glanced around, the first thing I noticed about the prison was that it was extremely neat, with rows of orange and pink impatiens planted along the walkway. It had the appearance of a well-kept community college. Everywhere women were sweeping and raking, or pretending to sweep and rake. I scrutinized them as I walked past. They didn't seem scary. They seemed bored and wary. As I walked up the carefully tended asphalt path, I became aware that the women were watching me as carefully as I was watching them. I smiled at each of the women as I passed. Most of them stopped their work and with faces set in stone followed me with their eyes, but one woman shyly smiled back. She worked her broom to the right of me and kept pace as I walked along, and she swept. I passed a building marked Orientation and another marked Clinic, and walked on toward the sign that indicated the chapel. In the distance, I saw an oval track where women were walking and jogging. To the left of me stood several large, concrete, dorm-looking buildings, about three stories high with no bars on the windows.

This federal prison had been, at one time, a boys' vocational school, which partly explained the layout. I had learned that in the seventies, it became an experimental co-ed prison. Not surprisingly, there were many unexplained pregnancies, and the experiment was terminated in 1990. The prison housed 1200 twelve-hundred women, although I didn't see nearly that many people milling around. Where was everybody, I wondered? My sweeper shyly pointed her broom at the building to the right of me. It was the chapel. I turned around to thank her, but she was gone. I headed toward the dark building with the double glass doors and walked inside.

At a desk, sat an inmate who greeted me with a big open smile. She was big-boned with a gap between her teeth and flyaway brown hair.

"Hey there. Are you the new chaplain?" she asked, standing up from her desk to greet me.

"Hi," I answered. "My name is Susan, and I'm the new chaplain intern." I offered my hand for her to shake, which she hesitantly took. (Although I had learned in Orientation not to use first names, I couldn't bring myself to reference myself as "Chaplain Pohl." That would take some time. I also learned that shaking hands was not done out of sanitary concerns.)

"Hello Chaplain. Nice to have you here."

"Is Chaplain Becker around?" I asked, not sure what else to say. She pointed me to the first office on the left, and then went back to her desk. I walked down the corridor and knocked on the office door. Chaplain Becker rose to greet me. He was polite and reserved. He appeared to be about fifty-five years old, slender, six feet tall and had thin wisps of gray hair that seemed a bit unmanageable. He wore a priest's collar and his shoulders were hunched forward as if warding off an attack. He had been in the prison system as a chaplain for more than thirty years. I smiled at him and introduced myself. He stared back at me with watery blue eyes and an inquisitive but unsmiling face. He got up and showed me the office that was designated for the interns.

"I'm glad you're here. There will be two other interns sharing the office with you but they haven't arrived yet. There really isn't much to show you. You can't have access to the computer because you're not an employee. You can't have access to the inmates' files for the same reason. There's a schedule for services in the sanctuary, which the secretary can go over with you. Would you like to see the sanctuary itself?"

I told him I would, and he led me across the hall. We entered through two large wooden doors flanked by tall rectangular windows. The room was A-framed with wooden beam cathedral ceilings, and beige carpeting. It had the secular plainness of a chapel in Las Vegas without the glitz. The overhead lighting fixtures, made of rectangular shaped polished brass, had a dainty etching on the outside of the glass panes. I wondered as if they had just been washed and polished that morning. A plain chancel occupied the front of the space and a pulpit sat to the side. A large homemade wooden table stood in front of the chancel. Someone had picked flowers from the outside garden and carefully arranged them in a plain glass vase that sat on the table. Chaplain Becker explained that the table was used as the altar for communion.

"The sanctuary is a multipurpose religious space that is used for all religious services," Chaplain Becker informed me. "Let me see, what else should I tell you? Oh, unfortunately, when you need to go to the bathroom, you'll have to come and ask me, or the secretary, for the key because we keep it continually locked. You could use the inmate's bathroom, but I don't recommend it. Once you go through key training, you can get your own key to the bathroom. You haven't done that yet have you?"

I shook my head no.

"Well, it's one of the things we need to schedule. A key to the chapel itself is out of the question, of course, because you can never be in here without a permanent staff member."

I nodded.

"What do you plan to do today?"

I stared at him blankly. Did he remember that today was my first day? I was feeling extremely anxious just being here and had not a clue about what I was supposed to do.

"I don't know. What do you think would be the most effective use of my time?"

"Effective use of your time," he repeated slowly. I realized that my question had a business sound to it, and I was here to do ministry. It was difficult to shake off my prior twenty-five years of human resources experience. What would a normal religious person ask?

"What I mean is what is the best way to carry out my ministry?" I asked correcting myself.

He brightened with that question, and actually smiled.

"What is your ministry?"

Answer a question with a question. If I knew what my ministry was, I would have the second half of my life figured out. Suddenly the answer came to me.

"Being here," I said with relief.

"Exactly," he almost beamed at me. "So here you are," he continued on in a jovial tone of voice, and with that, I swear to God, he walked back to his office. What was I supposed to do exactly?

I followed him back into his office.

"Uh, Chaplain Becker," he turned from his computer to face me.

"Is there something that I could read to orient me to the institution? Something that might help me to assimilate into the role of chaplain?"

He stared at me without answering, for what seemed like five minutes.

"I'm trying to decide how much of your anxiety I should take on," he finally said.

He got up from his computer, walked over to his bookshelf and pulled down a five-inch binder.

"Here are the policies of the institution. You can read these if you like," he said as he handed over ten pounds of paper.

I thanked him and walked back to the intern office. Now what? Read all of these policies? As a former human resources person, I knew just how much the policies were worth. I decided to check out the office I had been assigned. There were Bibles in English and Spanish that filled the two-shelf, gray, metal bookcase that lined one wall. A computer, that I couldn't use, sat on top of a gray metal desk. There were no religious icons in the office, only a poster that had all of the Christian religions on it with explanations of their theology and history.

A see-through glass window filled the wall between my office and the secretary's office. I guess this was a way to keep track of everyone. The secretary wasn't there, so I couldn't talk to her about schedule.

I had decided to go ask the chaplain another question, when a six-foot-two African American woman came out of the sanctuary and banged on the frame of the office door.

"I need a chaplain," she yelled. For a moment, I was totally petrified. I walked toward the door and tried to walk around her.

"Um, just a minute. Let me see if Chaplain Becker is here." I said with the intent to find her a "real" chaplain.

"Can you help me or not?" she shouted into my face. I stood in front of her, made my decision, and let her into the office closing the office door behind her.

"I need myself a chaplain right now. I don't know if I can take this," with that comment, she dissolved into tears, covering her face with her large hands.

The woman's change from rage to grief shocked me. She sat in the small folding chair, most of her body falling off on one side or the other. Her face was as round and large as a dinner plate and shiny from the tears that covered her cheeks. I sat back down in the office chair, staring at her, helplessly. At first all she did was cry. Not knowing what else to do, I waited for her to settle down and offered her a tissue from the box that sat on the desk. She took the tissue and her eyes met mine.

"I just don't think I can take it here no more. I went off to mental but they told me they didn't have time for me and that I should come over here and talk to a chaplain. I just can't take it no more. I miss my mama."

I was a bit bewildered. Mental? Missing her mama? I fell back on reflective listening techniques I had learned in management classes.

"You miss your mama?"

"Indeed, I do. She was the only one, the only one, who ever loved me. She loved me and cherished me, and now she's gone," and with that this large woman, who had frightened me, started to sob.

"When did you find out about your mama?" I asked.

"Find out what?" she asked me clearly perplexed.

"Find out that she was gone."

"The chaplain told me she passed. I couldn't go to her funeral or nothing because I didn't have the money to pay the guards. I can't believe she's gone." Her whole body shook with sobs.

"Did she die recently?"

"Yes ma'am, she died a year ago today."

"Was your mother religious?" I asked, still having no idea what to say or do.

"Yes, ma'am. She was a proud member of the Holiness Church."

Now what, I wondered. For some reason, I thought of music.

"Was there a hymn she liked to sing?" I asked hoping it would be a hymn I knew.

"Yes ma'am, she loved "Jesus Loves Me.""

"Well, how about if we sing that for your mother?" The woman agreed and we sang, "Jesus Loves Me" several times, me hesitantly at first, aware of my weak voice. She had a strong beautiful voice, (I learned later that she sang in the chapel choir) and she sang slowly and with deep feeling as I hesitantly accompanied her.

At the end of our singing, she stood up and seemed calmer.

"I usually go to mental, but they sent me over here. I just don't know if I can take it. I miss my mama so much," and with that she left the office.

I breathed a sigh of relief that I had survived my first contact with an inmate.

I went to search for Chaplain Becker to tell him what had happened.

He was sitting in his office in front of his computer and waved me in as I stood at his door. I described what had happened with the inmate, and then told him that I had some questions. He nodded for me to go ahead.

"When she said she usually went to "mental," what did she mean?" I asked as I sat down.

"That's what the inmates call going to the psychology building. They must have been busy if they sent Ms. Johnson over here."

"Do you know her?" I asked.

"Yes," he answered with a slight smile.

"Well, what do you think of how I handled the situation?" I asked.

"What do you think of how you handled it?" I took a deep breath in order not to scream at him.

"I don't know. It was all I could think of. Do you think she's ok?"

He said nothing.

"I guess I'm worried because she said she couldn't take it."

"Do you think she's suicidal?" he asked.

"I don't know," I answered trying to keep the sound of panic out of my voice. "How would I know that?"

"Did you ask her?"

"No," I replied feeling a bit guilty.

"Well maybe you can track her down on the compound and ask her."

"Ask her if she is suicidal?"

"Sure. Why not?" he asked, with a quizzical look on his face.

"I don't know it just seems…impolite," I responded hesitantly.

"Impolite? You're worried that you might be impolite if you ask an inmate if she is considering suicide?" I gave him one of his expressionless stares in return.

"How about this?" he decided to help me out. "Are you worried that if you ask her if she's suicidal that it will put the idea in her head?"

"Yes. I guess I am," I said realizing that what he said was true.

"Well, don't be," he said in a reassuring voice. "It's a common but irrational fear that people have about people who are suicidal. You can't make a person commit suicide just by asking them the question," he said.

"Ok," I said with relief. "I'll go find her and ask her if she is suicidal, but what if she says she is? What do I do then?"

"We put her in the clinic on a twenty-four hour hold," he said matter-of-factly.

"How will I find her?"

Chaplain Becker turned around input her name in his computer and said, "Residence Unit A. It's just across the way from here. You can find it," he smiled at me as he returned to his work.

I learned later that Chaplain Becker believed in experiential learning. He believed the only way to deal with fears and anxieties about a system as complex and oppressive as the prison system was to confront them directly. He also knew most of the inmates on the compound by name, and had known Ms. Johnson for several years through her participation in the chapel's choir, and presumed from my description that she was not suicidal.

I walked out of the chapel and began to search for Ms. Johnson.

I walked across the compound toward the dormitory units. I had no idea where I was going, how I was going to find her, or what I was going to say once I did find her. My anxiety on a scale of one to ten was about a twelve. There were no people on the compound, and I wondered again where everyone was. Although the compound was empty, I still felt the tension in the air once I left the chapel. There were several guards, or as they preferred to be called, officers, who crossed the path in front of me walking with a clear sense of purpose. I felt uneasy realizing that I was walking across a prison compound on my own. Although everything appeared calm and peaceful on the surface, I was hyper-vigilant as I walked across the compound.

I quickly found Unit A, walked up to the glass door, pulled the handle, and found that the door was locked. One of the officers came to the door, checked my badge and said that the units were only open during "open movement." I had no idea what that was, but asked if Ms. Johnson were in the unit. She scanned through her list and said, "Yes. This is her unit. Do you want to come in?"

I hesitated. I didn't really want to go inside, but this is what I had signed up for. I took a deep breath and said yes.

I walked into the building. The space seemed nothing like the prisons I had seen on television. It appeared to be more like what it had been years ago, the lobby of a dormitory. It had floor to ceiling glass windows that flooded the area in natural light. Plastic tables and chairs were arranged haphazardly on a brown linoleum covered floor. Against the back of the lobby, an open stairway led to a second floor. Upstairs, the rooms lined up on one side of a walkway that overlooked the lobby.

"The rooms are all open," the officer informed me. "You can go upstairs and see if she's there. She's in room 215."

I climbed the stairs and noticed inmates sitting inside their rooms. They were chatting to one another, but fell silent as I walked by. Room 215 appeared empty. I knocked on the doorframe and then entered. I was curious as to what the rooms were like inside.

The first thing that greeted me was a toilet sitting out in the open. A small sink and mirror were located on the wall to the right of the toilet. The rooms were originally designed to house one person, but because of the overcrowding, (when the facility was designed in 1974 it was built to house 250 people and now housed over twelve-hundred people) the rooms usually contained three or sometimes four women. I continued to inspect the room and saw that there were two sets of bunk beds placed on the back wall with a small rectangular window between them.

I later learned that each woman had a footlocker for her belongings that she could lock when she left the room. The rooms themselves were always left unlocked and could only be locked from the outside by one of the guards. The use of the toilet was a scheduled event that often resulted in conflict among the four women. Showers were located down the hall. There was no sign of Ms. Johnson or her roommates. I walked back downstairs to the lobby, and told the officer that no one was in the room. The officer shrugged and said she was probably programmed somewhere. I nodded, as if I understood, and she opened the door to let me out.

I walked back across the compound toward the chapel. Prison was not what I thought it was going to be. It seemed more like a reform school for women. There were no bars on the doors, with screaming people as I walked by. The toilet thing was disgusting, and the thought of four women living in that small space seemed inhumane. Still the grounds were pretty and clean. There were many things that I didn't understand.

When I returned to the office, I was happy to see that the secretary was in. I expected that she would be more forthcoming about life on the compound. She was very sweet and helpful. She told me that open movement was scheduled every hour for fifteen minutes. During this time, the inmates could move from building to building. No inmate was allowed on the compound unless it was open movement or they had a job as groundskeeper. This explained the lack of people in the open areas. The secretary suggested I sit in the lobby to wait and see if Ms. Johnson would show up asking for me, which she thought seemed likely. I went back to the lobby, and sat down on one of the couches and watched the comings and goings during open movement.

As I sat watching people, a young American Indian girl sat down on the cushion next to me. She had a broad face, beautiful skin, and long dark hair pulled into a ponytail that she flipped from side to side and wrapped and unwrapped around her finger.

"I suppose you think it's easy being a drug dealer," she said by way of introduction. I was taken aback by her question. I had been staring out the doors, intently searching for Ms. Johnson, and had not really acknowledged her.

"Well, no," I responded, thinking that this would cut off the conversation.

"You're damn right it isn't easy. Pardon me. Now take me. My family business is a chop shop that we run outta' the back of the rez', but I didn't want to do that. I wanted to do my own thing, see?" I nodded, as I continued to search for Ms. Johnson.

"First of all, there's the matter of phones. Do you know how many cell phones you have to have, switching them out all the time? I never used my personal phone. I was always careful. Didn't do my business near my home either. I kept a close watch so no one could get close to me. It's a mean business. You gotta' deal with crazy people, addicts. They'd slice your head off without even knowing what they're doing."

"Did you do drugs?" I asked rather timidly, hooked by her story in spite of myself.

"No. I told you it was a business," she turned toward me with a scowl on her face. "I wouldn't take that shit, pardon me." I nodded at her.

"Anyway, like I was telling you, you have the suppliers who are on you all of the time, telling you to sell more, break up your product and get it out there. Then you have the addicts, who are nuts. Then you got the stupid cops who you think are bought off and then they're not, and then on top of that you have other people trying to break into your territory. The competition is just waiting for you to fall, make a mistake. Just cause I'm young and female, I'm nineteen, did you know that? Anyway, they think they can take advantage 'cause I'm a girl. They think maybe I'm soft. Had to put that one down quick." She paused and we both watched as women came and went from the lobby. An older Asian woman came in, sat down, and took two large knitting needles out of her bag and started to knit. They allow her to have long knitting needles but told me I couldn't bring a stapler in?

"Nineteen years old, and I have been to places I can't even pronounce," she started talking again without any response from me. "I never thought I'd leave the reservation much less end up in some place like Thailand. We were laughing our asses off when I was told to fly there. We didn't know where in the hell it was, pardon me. Had to find a map big enough to find the place. Took forever to fly there. Once you get there, you got to make sure the stuff you're buying is the real deal. Then you got to make sure the mules that bring it back are gonna be straight up with you." As she continued to talk, I was overcome by how little I knew about her world. Was this assignment totally impossible? Should I have just waited until an internship spot came open at another one of the hospitals? Isn't that what I was really called to do? She continued on, oblivious of my crisis of sense of call.

"My family thinks just because the chop shop requires heavy lifting and chopping the cars up, that the boys' work is harder than mine," she continued. "I get no respect from my family. Here I was, one of the biggest dealers in the west, making more money than all of them put together. They took my cash, sure, but they disrespected me. It's always about the boys. Listen, every day, I had to watch my own back. Knowing one day they'd get me. My family was no help. They probably turned me in for the reward money. Watch your back. People told me that. I knew it, too. When you're making that kind of money, you better watch your back, girl. That's what they said. Somebody'll get you. Won't take long. I had to watch my own back." She sat quietly for a moment. "Guess I didn't watch close enough."

I was about to say something inane, when Ms. Johnson walked in through the double doors.

"Excuse me a minute," I said to the young woman, who barely gave me a nod.

Ms. Johnson appeared frightened.

"They said you been looking for me. That right?" she asked as she rushed up to me. As we walked back to the intern office, I told her I was glad to see her.

We sat down and she stared at me with no expression on her face.

"Ms. Johnson, when you were here earlier today, you said you couldn't take it. Is that right?"

"That's right ma'am. I miss my mama so bad," and she started to cry again.

"Well, do you miss her so bad that you might do something?" She suddenly stopped crying and peered up at me.

"What you mean do something?" she paused clearly confused. I didn't say anything.

"You mean do me some harm? You mean like to kill myself?"

"Yes, Ms. Johnson; I am worried about that."

"Well, Chaplain, I'd never do that, 'cause then I'd never get to see my mama. Uh uh." She stood up, and shook her head at me.

"You scared me to death. When the chaplain comes a callin', it ain't never good news. You done scared me to death," she pronounced as she left the office.

I decided she wasn't suicidal.

I sat back down at the desk and started to rummage through the drawers, wondering if I would find anything of interest or that could point me in some direction. I heard a quiet tap at the door, and in walked Lori my fellow intern that I had met at orientation.

"Oh, my God, Lori. I am so glad to see you. You'll not believe the weirdness that is going on here."

"What?" Lori asked with a little girl giggle as she sat in the church chair by the door.

"So what happened to you this morning? Did you hug someone or give them a Skittle?" she asked, and we both laughed in relief.

I began to tell her about the morning, when Chaplain Becker came knocking on the door and told us it was time for our theological group reflection.

There were three chaplain interns who were assigned to the prison as part of the Clinical Pastoral Education program or CPE. The very initials make sturdy theologians shiver. CPE explains its mission as saying that it approaches learning for the caregiver and caretaker as human living documents. The philosophy of CPE is that you must understand yourself and be able to care for yourself before you can extend your hand to help and to understand others. Part of the CPE requirements demand that a chaplain have been in therapy, and they must get a reference of approval to attend CPE training. If you are thinking this is a touchy-feely experience, you are in the wrong aisle of the bookstore. This is group therapy with a theological basis. Although it sometimes feels like it is an endurance contest it is designed to provoke students to see what they understand about themselves and their theology. As a seminary student, it is all part of the formation process. The supervising pastor, in this case Chaplain Becker, has the responsibility to listen to and reflect on the deepest meaning of the interns' interactions. This is not a time for pat answers or recycled religious dogma that has no personal meaning. The supervisor is expected to push the seminary students to clarify their theology and help them understand what it's like to practice in the secular world.

This push to have the intern clarify their theology can, at times, feel like a confrontational scene from group therapy.

Chaplain Becker had called the three chaplains into our first group meeting. The group consisted of Chaplain Becker; Chaplain Gerber, the other staff chaplain who worked at the prison; the other two chaplain interns, Lori, and Margaret; and me. The five of us sat in Chaplain Becker's office, where there was barely space for our five chairs. We sat quietly waiting for someone to start.

"I think we should start with prayer," Margaret began.

"Go ahead," Chaplain Becker answered.

Margaret prayed and we sat there again in silence.

"Well, what are we going to do now?" Margaret asked.

"What do you want to do?" Chaplain Becker replied.

"I think we should decide what type of work each of us is going to do, and what our schedules should be, and divide up our office time," she answered.

None of us responded. We sat in silence again for a few more minutes.

"I wonder if you two male chaplains find it difficult to work in a women's prison?" Lori asked.

The two men then began a discussion about the difficulties of being surrounded by women all day, and how it was difficult for them. They had both worked in men's prisons prior to their current assignment and believed that the women were more emotionally demanding than the men. The three of us women nodded our heads in agreement and understanding.

"Would anyone like to begin by discussing an interaction with an inmate?" Chaplain Becker turned the discussion back to us. Since Lori and Margaret had just gotten to the prison, I knew that the question was aimed at me. I told them about Ms. Johnson, her anger turning to tears, my feelings of helplessness, singing with her, and then going to find her to make sure that she was not suicidal.

"So what was your theological position when Ms. Johnson started to cry about the death of her mother," Chaplain Gerber asked me.

I was raised a Southern Baptist, but I left that tradition long ago. As I was soon to find out, my theology was often still grounded in a faith and beliefs I held as a child. I now belong to the Unity denomination, which is big on spirit and prayer but not so big on theology. Unity theology can be summed up with "God is absolute good everywhere present." I didn't know how that theology was going to help me with the chaplain's question or my time in this prison for that matter. I found myself wildly searching to have an inkling of an idea of my real theology in the moment with Ms. Johnson. I finally gave up.

"I have no idea what my theological stance was. I know that I felt helpless. I wanted to comfort her, and didn't want to piss her off, and I wanted her to stop crying. I thought she was probably a fundamentalist, and that she would like to sing."

"So you were trying to pacify her?" Chaplain Gerber asked.

"I don't know if I were trying to pacify her. Maybe."

"I guess I'm curious as to why you reverted to your childhood faith as an approach with her?" Chaplain Becker looked at me with curiosity.

"I thought her faith was the same as mine as a kid, and it was a way to try to communicate with her, to try to make a connection with her."

"I understand that," Chaplain Becker said, "but what about your faith? Are you going to change your faith based on every inmate you meet? That could be quite a challenge."

We all sat there for a moment contemplating that reality.

The faith of my childhood came back to me in a rush.

Chapter Two

TENT REVIVALS
AND SNAKE HANDLERS

---

*God and I go way back. The first time he talked to me, he was bossy, as
usual, telling people when to come and go. I was hiding among the clouds,
when I heard his voice deep in my heart, "Susan, time to go. The family
is down there waiting for you." I peered down and saw a slender blonde
woman, with a bulging stomach hanging white sheets up on a clothesline.
A red-haired girl stood next to her, carefully lifting the sheets up from the
clothesbasket and handing them to the woman, who pinned them to the
line. The clothesline was set up on a perfectly mowed patch of green grass. A
blue swing set and teeter-totter filled out the yard. The smell of lilacs drifted
up, and I felt the sweet appeal of a June day in Michigan. The family
seemed normal enough, but then they always do. I glanced up at God to tell
him I wasn't quite ready, that I had one more thing I needed to...*

I was born June 29, 1946 at four o'clock in the afternoon at a
hospital in Trenton, Michigan.

That's the story I told the family when I was three years old
anyway, and we have all believed it ever since.

I was born with a gift of faith; in my life, sometimes it
has shown itself to be a type of faith that could move mountains,
and other times it couldn't move a dust ball. The house God sent
me to was in Lincoln Park, Michigan, a small suburban city, down-
river from Detroit. Life with the new family was not exactly what
I had pictured while floating up in the sky next to God. True, it
had a perfect yard, with swings and room to run and play tag, and

an older little girl lived there, but something felt wrong in the house. A heaviness of spirit blanketed the rooms, and the older girl was constantly watchful, as if something really bad was going to happen at any moment. Also, if I were the answer to my mother's prayer, my new sister Diane didn't feel the same. My mother had promised her a playmate, like six-year-old Kathy who lived down the street. When Diane glanced into my crib I let out a ferocious wail, she said to my mother, "Take her back." That was pretty much her attitude toward me for the next eighteen years.

My mother seemed precariously balanced, and had little patience for children who were not perfectly behaved. No matter how much we tried, either Diane or I would make a mistake and then Mother would fly into a rage. She and Diane would often argue violently, and I learned to play in my room and stay away from both of them. I was very lonely. I missed God, the clouds, and the feeling of blissful harmony.

Then, when I was three and a half years old, God gave me a special Christmas gift. On December 26th, a new human spirit came into our home. Her name was Sarah. I fell in love with her from the first moment I gazed into her crib. We had Christmas pictures of baby Jesus lined up on the mantle of our fireplace, but I had my own baby, not in a manger, but in a wooden crib, painted with baby lambs and elephants. At three and a half, I was just about eye level with her as I peered through the wooden slats of her crib. As I stood next to her, I could feel her breath as it blew across my cheek. I loved the smell of her baby sleepers. I would hold the newly laundered clothes against my skin and inhale the smell of Ivory Flakes laundry detergent. I stood next to the crib for what seemed like hours waiting for her to wake up.

When she did open her eyes, she would find me, and smile at me as if I were the most amusing toy in her toy box. Sarah brought joy into my life then as she does now.

The church I was brought up in was Southern Baptist and, unlike my two sisters, I took everything that they said literally.

One Monday morning as I was walking to my elementary school, I began thinking about church the day before. The Sunday school lesson was based on the rapture, a theological concept that was a little advanced for a seven-year-old, but I pondered the harsh realities of it nonetheless. In Sunday School, the teacher said that very soon the end of the world would come, and those who were God's children would quickly be whisked up to heaven, with Jesus, a lamb, angels, and trumpets. I still remembered heaven, and I found the idea very appealing. Our Sunday school teacher, Mrs. Pearl, artfully demonstrated this weighty theological subject of the rapture on a flannel board with cutout paper pieces of Jesus, children, and a sleepy baby lamb that she carefully placed in Jesus' arms. Cherubic angels and trumpets festively decorated the sides of the board. As Mrs. Pearl slapped each character onto the board, they magically clung there just as we were told to cling to the love of Jesus.

Mrs. Pearl said that the rapture was coming soon and we needed to accept Jesus as our personal savior, but we had all done that in first grade, so I wasn't sure what we were supposed to be doing to ensure we would be raptured. I had previously asked my teacher about Sarah, my baby sister, being that she was only four years old and was not old enough to be saved. Would she be left behind, as she was when I started kindergarten? My teacher assured me that God would take all of the babies and little children with him to heaven. This was a big relief.

The thing that currently troubled me was whether I should have left a note to my mother that morning before I left for school, or would she know that I had floated up to God with Jesus and the rest of the chosen. I hadn't seen any mothers on the flannel cloth board, only the children, the lamb, the angels, and Jesus, so it seemed unlikely my mother would join me. I wasn't so sure about Diane, my older sister, either. I would ask her if she had been saved, but she would only glare at me with bright green eyes and tell me to shush. Since she had entered junior high school, she seemed to know everything about everything, so I had decided not to worry about her either.

At the ten o'clock recess period I felt pretty sure that if Jesus were going to show up that day, he would do it then, in order not to disturb school more than he had to. I walked out past the black-top of the playground, and ventured into the grass of the baseball field. I carefully tucked my green plaid dress underneath me, sat down, crossed my legs, and waited. Every time a cloud drifted by (in Michigan there are many drifting clouds), I would wonder if that were Jesus or if that were the beginning of the lamb breaking through the sky. I wasn't sure if Jesus would be moving, or if he would float down like a Polaroid picture that came spurting out of the bottom of my father's new camera. I thought maybe Jesus couldn't use his arms or legs, since all the photos of him showed him very still and stiff or flying straight up through the air without wings or anything.

I had seen many photographs of Jesus in the Baptist church and had inspected each of them carefully. The photo of him in profile staring out of a stained glass window and looking up to the sky seemed to be a personal favorite of the church, as it could be found in each of the wood paneled Sunday school rooms. In this picture, Jesus was turned sideways and had a big bright circle around his head, carefully combed red wavy hair (similar to my sister Diane's, although no one else but me seemed to notice it), a neatly trimmed goatee, and wearing his regular long white robes. Other photos showed him carrying a lamb, again with perfectly laundered white Jesus robes and the same haircut. I wondered if Jesus ever got dirty because his clothes were always so clean. Because we were Baptists, our church had a picture of Jesus being baptized in a river with a dove coming down over his head and a spooky sky that opened to show that God was up there somewhere. Other, more gruesome pictures showed Jesus on a cross, with his clothes in shreds, but the Baptists didn't really approve of those, so I could put any Jesus-on-the-cross thoughts out of my head. Pictures of the baby Jesus in the manger weren't that helpful, either, because I couldn't imagine Jesus bringing the manger, the cows, the donkeys, the shepherds, and the wise men with him when he came to take us to heaven. That left me with the floating Jesus who would probably just drift down. It was important to be alert, as he could probably be mistaken for a cloud or a tree branch. I sat intently staring at the sky.

"Susan, what are you doing out here?" I almost jumped out of my skin, but it was not a divine apparition, only my second grade teacher Mrs. Edmonds.

"Didn't you hear the recess bell? What in the world are you doing way out here sitting by yourself? Are there any other kids or adults out here?" she asked suspiciously. "Are you ok? Why didn't you come in when the bell rang?"

"I'm waiting for Jesus."

"You're doing what?" Mrs. Edmonds turned to me with alarm.

"I'm waiting for Jesus, the angels, the lamb, and the trumpets. He's going to take all of the children to heaven. I learned about it yesterday in Sunday school."

She paused to consider this piece of religious prophecy.

"What church do you go to?" she finally asked very slowly.

"First Baptist church on Fort Street." I said proudly. Mrs. Edmonds frowned, clearly in some kind of adult conundrum.

"Well, they didn't mention any such rapture at my church, St. James Episcopal Church, and I think it's quite safe for you to now return to your classroom."

I didn't mention to her that my mother said that the Episcopal Church was based on divorce and a desire to drink wine, so it seemed to me that Episcopalians were unlikely to have a thorough understanding of something like the rapture. Mrs. Edmonds seemed to think the matter of Jesus, the lamb, the children, the angels and the trumpets was closed, and she scooted me back into the classroom. It was the first time that I had come across differences of dogma in the church, but it certainly would not be the last.

Being Southern Baptists, we spent a lot of time in church. On Sunday, we had Sunday school, regular service, and Voice of Christian Youth on Sunday night. Monday was Christian women's meeting. Tuesday was missionary meeting night. Wednesday was prayer meeting. Thursday was men's night (I didn't go to that), and we were off Friday, for high school football games, and Saturday to prepare for Sunday. Then the week started all over again. I thought it imperative for the family's soul that we attend all of the church services, but this, surprisingly was met with a bit of resistance. Diane was impossible. I begged her to go with me every night, and I explained to her that it might mean temporary discomfort now, but her mortal soul was at stake. (This is what the preacher had said the week before.) After a particularly impassioned plea explaining to her the harrowing fate of those who were not saved, I heard Diane in the kitchen arguing with my mother.

"Mother, I am not going to church every day of the week. Sunday service at eleven is enough. I have homework to do. If Susan wants to go to every single service, every single night, she can just go by herself. One religious nut in this family is enough." With these words, Diane stomped out of the kitchen. I was sure that Mother would side with the church and me, but I was disappointed. Although salvation was something my mother cared about, she had two other unfortunately conflicting principles that governed her life. One was the idea of freedom of choice, and the second was the importance of schoolwork. Diane ended up attending the eleven o'clock Sunday service only. My mother also thought that since she had been saved many years ago, that the Sunday service would suffice for her as well.

This left my dad, who was born an Italian Catholic, of all things, as a special target for my evangelistic zeal. He was often at work, and so he got excused for all but Sunday service. Sarah and I were the only ones left to hold up the family honor in church attendance. Sarah wasn't particularly religious either; in fact, she thought the whole thing was merely an opportunity to wear pretty dresses, and chat with her friends. Being the youngest, she of course, graciously agreed to accompany me to all of the services. I was sure I would be able to convert Sarah before too long, but she was still too young to really count.I considered this conversion challenge very important because of a Sunday school competition going on. Each Sunday, we received a little, personalized pamphlet. The front showed a very appealing picture of Jesus standing on terra firma with a lamb slung around his shoulders. In our little book, we had to keep count of how many people we had talked to about Jesus (I usually counted my entire second grade class.); whether or not we had read our Sunday school lesson, this was an easy check mark; and whether we had memorized our Bible verse. Check mark and gold star number three. My problem was the last question on the list. How many conversions did we make during the week? You couldn't get four gold stars unless you had a conversion. This was really difficult for me because everyone I knew, other than my sisters, had already been converted. Barbara Brown, my evangelical nemesis got four gold stars every week. It was really unfair because she lived in an area where no one went to church, and she could get conversions with the snap of a finger. She was known to drag in five new people at a time and bring them to Sunday school. I was sure she was bribing them with candy, but I couldn't prove it. My only hope lay with Sarah.

After church, I told Sarah I needed to practice my preaching skills, thinking that hearing the sermon the second time would do her good. Although she wasn't keen on sitting through another church service, she eventually agreed, once Mom said she could keep her pink-lace dress on until I finished practice church. Once we had settled into our bedroom, I took all of Sarah's dolls off the shelf, lined them up on little chairs, put Sarah in the middle, and repeated the sermon as I recalled it. I thumped the Bible and tried to get all of the sounds just right. I asked for Sarah's critique of both the sermon and hymn selections that I made. Sarah's advice about my sermon was always the same; make the sermon shorter and have more singing. I thought ten minutes was the absolute minimum for a sermon. Sarah insisted that five minutes should suffice. We settled in the middle with a seven-minute sermon. Although it was a trial for me to get across all of my theological beliefs in seven minutes, that was absolutely as long as Sarah, and the rest of my parishioners, would stay.

One day, after hearing how anyone who was not baptized in the faith would go to hell, and losing one more Sunday school lesson to Barbara Brown, I became worried about Sarah's bride doll collection that had joined us for the "after church service." I wasn't sure if Sarah's dolls had been saved, in spite of the fact that they had sat through all of my sermons. I decided that they had enough religious training to be taken into the faith, and I had aspirations of five new conversions. I propped up her five bride dolls on the bed, and asked them if they accepted Jesus as their personal savior, and they seemed to be in unison in their response. I was rapturous. While Sarah was outside playing, I took each doll, and in the Baptist tradition, carefully dunked each one in the bathtub while reciting the Lord's Prayer. As they came up, each of the bedraggled bride dolls seemed to have a spiritual glow. I carefully lined them up on Sarah's drawer and waited for her to see how happy the dolls were, knowing that their souls were protected for eternity.

Unfortunately, my sister did not fully comprehend the stakes of salvation, and when she saw her dolls, she let out a bloody scream that pierced my ears. Mother came running, thinking that one of us had killed the other. She took one look at the dolls, Sarah's red hollering face, and me and said, "Susan, quiet her down," and she left.

"Sarah, I can't believe you are having such a fit! I have just saved your dolls' souls, presuming they had one. You should be thrilled." Sarah's wailing continued unabated. She could be extremely dramatic when she wanted.

I tried to reason with her, "Sarah, the dolls will dry out but their souls could be lost forever, but now they're saved." I started to cry myself at the thought of it all. She finally noticed that I was crying too, and said, without much caring, I must admit.

"You are a lunatic. Don't you ever do that again. These are my dolls, and I get to say what they do."

I thought that this was probably a good point, and decided not to carry out my plans for her Barbie Dolls of the World collection.

One of the things that Southern Baptists do in the summer is have revivals, because preaching to the same people, after everybody has already been saved, was redundant, even for a Baptist. Plus, church attendance would go down in the summers because people would take off on vacations or devise other ways of escape. Even I became a bit lethargic in my evangelical zeal, during the hot, humid months of July and August in Michigan. To combat this religious apathy, churches held tent revivals, where people would come forward and be revived in the Spirit. People were healed of all kinds of illnesses, and some said that people could be raised from the dead. Even though my mother pooh-poohed it all, I was certain that I could have a true religious experience, and learn how to heal people if I could get to the tents at night.

My mother was inclined to let me go, but my father, who always said yes to everything, was suddenly unsure if I should be allowed to go without any family members. I begged him, and told him that I would be quiet and that nothing could possibly go wrong in the safety of a church tent. There were people from our church who would be going, and I promised to walk to the tent service and back home with them. Sarah, having heard that some fools might be handling snakes, refused to go, and wouldn't let her dolls go either. I was once again on my own on the road to salvation.

The first great thing about the tent revivals was that different preachers would come every night, so I could study their preaching style. The tent sat on the black asphalt of the church parking lot. On hot nights, the flaps of the tent could be raised to let a breeze drift through. The audience was made up mainly of the people who attended the First Baptist Church in Lincoln Park. As you walked into the tent, you could pick up photocopies of mimeographed pages of the songs that we would sing that night. There were also special 3x5 prayer cards to be filled out for anyone who had special prayer needs. The audience frequently used the sheet music and the cards to slowly fan themselves as they sat through the service on the hot, sticky nights.

All of the evangelists were popular, but one was so great that he stayed a whole week. His name was Reverend Peter, and his singing voice rattled the metal poles of the tent. He never used a microphone when he spoke to us. Instead, he would walk down the aisle, with all of us sitting on our fold up metal chairs, and get right up close in our face so you could see his big white teeth and smell the cologne on his hair. I was in heaven. He had a cadence when he preached that was better than a drum beat.

"And this, I tell you," he preached with his voice rising to the tent tops, "is the true word of God for anyone who will listen." As he preached, he thumped his Bible to the rhythm. He sounded just like God himself. It was so inspiring. He sang hymns that we all knew, such as "When the Roll Is Called Up Yonder," and we sang at the top of our lungs into the hot Michigan night. When Reverend Peter preached, I forgot about the heat, the fact that my legs stuck to the hard metal chair and about the homework that was due the next day. I could have sat in the humid heat all night long to listen to Reverend Peter.

At the end of Reverend Peter's talk, he gave a very emotional altar call. (This is when you go up to the altar or the makeshift altar and accept Jesus as your personal savior. After that you are saved for eternity.) He started real slow and soft as he led into his call.

"I just want one person, here in the audience, to make one small step for Jesus." He said this so quietly, that you could hardly hear him after all of the thumping. Shockingly, no one came forward. Then Reverend Peter would get a little louder and plead, "Isn't there one person out there who will make one small step for Jesus? He then started to cry. The pianist was playing "Just as I Am," which is a hymn that would tug on the devil's own heart. I was crying just thinking of the potential of all of the lost souls.

"I am telling you that I have been called to preach the gospel and not one of you will come forward? Just one person, please take a step for Jesus," and then he started to sob. Well, I thought I could make one small step for Jesus. So I got up from my metal chair and walked the aisle up toward the front of the tent. Reverend Peter said, "And so a little child shall lead them." Before you knew it, there were tons of other people with me at the altar. The gathering sang "Blessed Assurance" and it was magical.

Reverend Peter was not only a good evangelist, but he also had healing powers that defied explanation. He would start the healing part of the service by asking us all to bring forward from our hearts the person who most needed healing. We would raise our hands, and the reverend's wife would go through the audience and select people. She would go up to someone, and ask them to whisper in her ear the name of the person who was sick and what their ailment was. Reverend Peter would go into a deep trance, and then miraculously he would say the name of the person who needed healing, and what their sickness was. We all said "Hallelujah" and then prayed for that person with all of our might. After the healing, they passed the collection basket and everyone gave what they could. We were all honored to have such an important healer come to our town.

Each night that Reverend Peter was in town, the service was pretty much the same. He would give his rousing sermon, do the miraculous healing, and then do the altar call. People were so shy that no one would come forward. The reverend would start to cry and then I would start to cry and go up to the altar. Then the reverend would say, "A little child should lead them," and then a whole bunch of people would come forward.

Friday night there were so many people at the altar that I stayed up front to make sure everyone had cards so they could fill out their mailing address for the reverend to contact them about future prayers. I was so busy helping people with their cards, that I hadn't noticed people in the back of the tent. As I was helping someone with their card, I looked up and saw my dad. I was so happy to see him, thinking that maybe he had come to the front of the altar to be saved. He seemed pretty serious, so I thought maybe this was the night that he would turn his back on his idolatrous Catholic upbringing.

"Reverend," my dad called to the preacher. "My name is Bill Darin and this is my little girl." I beamed with pride, thinking how great this was that this was my dad's moment of salvation.

"How do you do Mr. Darin, so nice to meet you." Reverend Peter put on his special, shining smile and reached out to shake my dad's hand.

"How long have you been in town?" my dad asked.

"Well, this is the final night for me in a one-week revival. Your little girl here is something special. Are you one of the Lord's children?" the reverend asked my dad.

I held my breath waiting for my dad's answer.

"Reverend, how many times should someone go to the altar in order to be saved?" This was very exciting, kind of like Jesus and the Pharisees. I noticed that the reverend wasn't looking at my dad and suddenly seemed a little uncomfortable.

"Well, you can only be saved once," the reverend answered. "But we can hear the call of the Spirit many times in our life." For some reason my dad glared at him, picked me up and walked out of the tent. On our way home, we had a real adult conversation.

"Daddy, were you there for the whole service?"

"Um hmm."

"I didn't see you. Where were you?"

"I was standing in the back, watching you."

"Didn't you think that Reverend Peter was thrilling? He's so different than our Pastor Riley. Pastor Riley is so boring. He stays up front and doesn't walk down the aisle. He sings boring songs nobody knows. Reverend Peter sings all the songs we learned at camp and everyone sings along because the words are so easy. He knows everything about everything and Daddy, he can even heal people long distance. All you have to do is get on his mailing list and send him some money and he can heal people through the mail."

"I like Pastor Riley," Dad said as he started to swing my arms high in the air.

"Well, yeah, I like him too, but he sure doesn't cry like Reverend Peter. Reverend Peter just wouldn't stop crying until I went up front. Isn't that something?

"Um hmmm."

After that summer, Reverend Peter never came back for the night tent revivals. It was a great sorrow of mine through the third grade.

When I was nine years old, my mother decided it was time for us to visit her family in the Appalachian Mountains of East Tennessee. My sister Diane, who was then fifteen, adamantly refused to go. Diane was a force of nature. Her red hair forewarned of an obstinate personality and a temper to match. Although Sarah and I were initially concerned about the reasons behind Diane's refusal to go, we decided it would probably be fun to go for a long ride in the car, and so we hopped in the backseat, oblivious to our fate.

The first problem of the trip was my dad. He had recently bought my mother a brand-new 1955 Chevy Bel Air convertible, and he couldn't wait to get the car out on the open road. He was an engineer for General Motors, and cars were his passion. Being Italian, he also believed that cars should be driven hard and put through their paces. "Like a horse," he used to say. "You have to show a car who's boss." My mother hated horses, and loved her car.

For her, the car was a thing of beauty with its yellow bottom, black roof and whitewall tires. She believed her car should be treated gently and carefully.

"Careful, Bill," Mother cautioned, as we backed out of the driveway. It was an expression that we heard at various pitches all along the way to Tennessee. From Lincoln Park, Michigan to Andersonville, Tennessee is about five hundred miles. In 1955, it took fifteen hours of driving time for a normal driver to complete the trip. My father did it in twelve. Even at that, in child time, it seemed like the trip lasted three months.

First, we had to get through Ohio, which has to be the longest, most boring state in the entire universe—nothing but fields, cows, and more fields—flat and boring. Sarah and I sat nestled in the backseat, placed like eggs in their cardboard cartons. Since this was the era before seat belts, my mother's solution to keep us in place was to jam towels, blankets, pillows, and clothes on either side of us. Packed in our cocoons, Sarah and I eventually dozed off to the whistling sound of the wind as it reverberated against the black convertible top. All went well until we hit Kentucky. This is the point where my father lost his mind. Suddenly, there were curves in the road. Dad hunched over the steering wheel, put his foot on the gas, and accelerated into each curve. The contents of the backseat, including Sarah and me, were thrown around wildly as the backseat of the car swayed uncontrollably with each curve.

"Hey," we squealed from underneath the pillows, sheets, and blankets.

"Careful, Bill," my mother said in a rising tone of voice, to no avail. My father had clearly become possessed by a demon and would not slow down. I am sure we were going eighty miles an hour.

"Help," Sarah cried, squirming beneath an avalanche of mother's antique quilts. I tried to disentangle her by pushing quilts and blankets right and left. Our only reprieve came during the few straight parts of the road. On the straightaway, we would rearrange ourselves along with the contents of the backseat and sit up straight, hoping our young lives would not end prematurely.

As we flew into Tennessee, roadside signs posted before every curve said "Prepare to Meet Thy Maker." I leaned over to ask Sarah what she thought it meant, but she looked a little green and couldn't respond.

"Mom, what do those signs mean? What does it mean to 'Prepare to Meet Thy Maker?" I leaned into the front seat to hear her answer.

"We are about to find out if your father doesn't slow down. Bill, for Christ's sake, slow down." I leaned back into my cubbyhole as the front seat continued their squabble. Was I prepared to meet my maker? Was this different than the rapture? Despite my better instincts, I persisted in my line of inquiry with my mother.

"Mom," I cried over the whistle, and the cursing in the front seat. "What should I do to be prepared?"

"For God's sakes, Susan, sit back and be quiet."

"Sarah," I whispered. "Do you think if I learn all of the books of the Old Testament, I'll be prepared?

"Uhhhhhhh" was her only response. She really didn't seem too good. She suddenly opened her eyes and roused herself.

"Daddy, I'm going to be sick," oh, no, not on me, the quilts, the blankets. My mother must have had the same thought.

"Bill, pull this car off the road, now." Dad quickly responded and the entire rocking car came to a screeching halt. Sarah jumped out of the back seat, and threw up her fried chicken lunch while we all stood and watched. It was not a pleasant sight.

My mother gave my dad a glare that could have scorched a hot stone.

"Are you happy now?" she asked. The rest of the trip was at a much slower and more manageable pace.

As we arrived at my grandmother's house, I was still pondering how to be prepared to meet my maker. After telling Grandma about the trip, the car, Dad turning into a demon, and Sarah throwing up, I finally got down to serious business.

"Grandma, I want to be prepared to meet my maker," Grandma, unlike my mother, perked up at this religious testimony.

"Well, now, we'll just see to that up at the church. You want to go with me to my church?" Grandma asked as she gave me a big hug.

"I do, Grandma. Let's go now. We have no time to waste," I answered with all sincerity.

"Ma," I heard my mother call from the kitchen. "I don't think you should take the girls up there."

"Why not?" Sarah asked, suddenly showing an interest in religious matters.

"Ma. I don't know if that's the place for the girls. It's kind of backwoods up there. Why don't you just take 'em next door to the church on the hill?" Mother said, ignoring Sarah.

"Dellie, there's not a bit of problem of me takin' 'em up there. They can go the Baptist church any ole time. Charlie said he'd pick us up in the mornin'. If they want to go, they ought to be able to go."

Sarah, suddenly remembering an adult conversation she had overheard went over to stand in front of Grandma.

"Do they have snakes, Grandma?" she asked Grandma staring her straight in the eye.

"Yes, darlin', but they keep 'em in a box," Grandma said trying to reassure her.

"I'm not going," came her tart reply.

Snakes? This could be the beginning of a true religious experience.

Sunday morning, my grandma and I were the only ones up and ready to go to church. One of the neighbors came to get us in a big old black Ford pickup truck. We bounced over gravel roads as the truck labored up the steep mountainside and back into the woods. It was a slow drive with the truck lurching up the hills and grinding through the gears. The road had big ruts and dust flew up behind us as we made our way through the green woods where the scent of honeysuckle blooms filled the air with a sweetness that overcame the dust blowing through the windows. We were totally alone on the road. This was the first time I had ever been to a place with no sidewalks and no paved roads. It seemed like a place from "Wild Kingdom," my favorite TV show. Around the next bend in the road, on the right hand side, a beautiful white painted church with a tall steeple stood by itself in a grove of trees.

"Grandma, is that your church?" I asked in amazement. "It's beautiful."

"Yes, darlin.' It's the Holiness Pentecostal Church of Tazwell Valley."

Once we got parked, I jumped out of the pickup and raced ahead of Grandma to the front of the church. I could hear the sound of music coming from the open church windows. Everyone knew my grandma and greeted her as Miz Lizzie. We finally got ourselves into the church and settled down in the hard wooden pews. It seemed much like our Baptist church at home but plainer. No fancy windows, no carpets on the floor, and no cushions on the pews. There was a rough-hewn pulpit in the front and a choir full of people clapping and singing "Oh Happy Day," as we walked into the church.

Grandma checked out the bulletin and pointed out the verse for the service: Mark 16: 17-18. I grabbed my Bible to find the verse. Sure enough, there it was,

And these signs shall follow them that believe: In my name shall they cast out devils; they shall speak with new tongues;

They shall take up serpents; and if they drink any deadly thing; it shall not hurt them; they shall lay hands on the sick, and they shall recover.

Snakes were going to be in this service! I started bouncing up and down next to Grandma. I was really excited but I realized I was also a little scared. I moved closer to my grandma, and felt the reassurance of her bony little hip next to mine as I snuggled to get as close as I could. As scared as I was, I was also on the edge of my pew wanting to see what would happen. It was more exciting than an episode of "Jungle Jim." Maybe I could add this to my sermon repertoire. First, the preacher welcomed everyone, and Grandma stood and proudly introduced me to the congregation. They all greeted me just as if I were a grownup. Then we had more singing, very happy songs. Sarah would really have liked this, I thought. She should have come.

Once the preacher started into his sermon, things started to get a little weird. Instead of walking down the aisle pleading for people to take a step for Jesus, the preacher got himself so worked up that he ran down the center aisle and then flew outside the open church doors. We could see him running all around the outside of the church through the side windows. He was making a whooping sound as he ran completely around the outside of the church. He came back inside the church, up the aisle and then ran back outside and did it all over again. All the while, people were clapping and saying "Hallelujah." I had never seen a grown man run so fast. He was running, and sweating, and hollering a noise I had never heard, and the whole congregation was clapping and singing. He finally ran back up to the pulpit and stayed there a moment. He stood quietly mopping his bald head with a large white handkerchief while he and the congregation caught their breath. A man in the front pew suddenly stood up and said the Spirit was upon him.

"Come on up here, Brother Dew," the preacher said, telling the man to come up to the pulpit.

Brother Dew joined the preacher and stood with his back to us. I couldn't tell what was going on up front as we were sitting toward the back of the church. Then, Brother Dew started swaying real slow and rocking sideways. He leaned to the left, and then slowly leaned to the right. I realized that Grandma and I were starting to sway with him. All of a sudden, he started hollering in a language I had never heard before. It was not English that was for sure. Something about him hollering in the weird language really spooked me. I felt my hair stand up on edge, and I wasn't so sure I wanted to see anything more. I wished I had stayed home with Sarah. The preacher started to translate what Brother Dew was saying. It was all about Jesus, and our salvation, and the blood that was shed for us. People were crying and sobbing all over the church. I guess I was about as scared as I've ever been. Then someone from the back of the church brought a big box forward toward the pulpit.

"Grandma, are the snakes in there?" But Grandma continued swaying and didn't seem to hear me.

Then the preacher recited the verses from the book of Mark. He asked Brother Dew if he believed, and if he was right with God. Brother Dew answered that he was. Then the preacher lifted the top off the box, and Brother Dew stuck his hand in there and pulled out a big squirming snake. After Brother Dew grabbed the snake out of the box, the preacher slammed the top of the box down quick as a wink so the other snakes couldn't get out. The congregation was crying and praising God as Brother Dew held the snake up in the air. The snake twitched and wiggled, but Brother Dew had a firm hand around the base of the snake's head. Everyone was swaying and praying, and then the preacher opened the box, and the snake got thrown in with the others, and it was over.

We ended the service with the hymn "Just as I Am," and some people went up front to rededicate their lives to Jesus. I was not tempted in the least to leave my grandma's side and go up there with that box of snakes, even it if was closed. I looked down at my arms, and I still had goose bumps all over me. I guess I'd had a religious experience, but I wasn't sure I ever wanted another one.

On the way home, I asked Grandma what kinds of snakes were in the box.

"I reckon they were copperheads this week. Do you know Charlie?" she asked and turned to the driver.

"No, ma'am. I didn't get close enough to check, but they were either copperheads or water moccasins, whichever he had."

It took me all the way back to Andersonville before my stomach settled down.

As we walked toward the house, Grandma turned to me to give me a warning.

"Don't you say nothing about them snakes, honey, or your mama won't ever let you come again."

We walked in the house, and everyone asked, "How was church?"

"Fine," we both replied.

Chapter Three

GRIEF

No one ever told me that grief felt so like fear.—C.S. Lewis, A Grief Observed

66 **S**o Chaplain Pohl, I understand that you were trying to make a connection with this inmate but again," Captain Becker brought me back into the group, "what about your faith? Are you going to change your faith based on every inmate you meet? That could be quite a challenge."

"Susan," Lori, my new best friend, stepped into the silence, "if you had it to do again, how would you put your current faith into action with that inmate?"

It was then that the light bulb went off for me. Just because most of the women in prison were evangelical, and I had come from an evangelical background, did not mean I needed to turn my adult faith upside down to meet theirs. My community of faith is Unity. One of Unity's beliefs is an expression, "I behold the Spirit of God in you." If I could maintain that mind set, that each woman had a spark of divinity in her, then I could use my faith in seeing the goodness at the core of their being. If I could maintain that belief, then I could be with these women whose lives were so different than my own, knowing that we both shared the God spirit within us. As Unity says, for some of us there is a small spark and for others a bonfire.

I smiled at Lori.

"If I had put my faith in action, I would have believed that God was in the interaction in the room with us. I wouldn't have felt so afraid, knowing that I couldn't make a mistake that couldn't be fixed. I would have spoken to Ms. Johnson about God's love being like her mother's love. I would have relaxed more, and I wouldn't have tried so hard to figure out what to do next."

We all took a deep breath and sat in silence for a moment. Chaplain Becker asked if any of us would like to help lead a grief group with Chaplain Gerber, and I volunteered. I had done grief work before, and felt that I could manage doing a group in prison. The psychology department asked us in to do a group for women who had experienced the death of a family member. Chaplain Gerber said that we could do the workshop together, but the planning of it would be my responsibility.

I developed a structured program on grief. I talked with Chaplain Gerber about the plan and he thought perhaps we should just sit in a circle and see what happened. I felt internally horrified. See what happens? Hello, we are in a prison, here, I don't exactly want to see what happens. I told him that I thought some structure would be helpful for the inmates. He told me it was my call, and I proceeded with my ideas. I planned a four-week session. In the first week, we would do brief introductions. After that, each person would tell her story about the person who had died, while the rest of us listened. Week two would be reading "The Mustard Seed," a Buddhist story about grief. The third week we would discuss the stages of grief and learn what helped each woman cope with loss. Finally, in the fourth week we would discuss forgiveness, facts about grief, and the role of religion. I had prepared about an hour per session, and hoped it would go smoothly.

At the first meeting, we had five women sign up for the group. I introduced Chaplain Gerber and myself, and said that we would be together for four weeks. We started with a moment of silence. I told the women that they were to speak about the person that they were grieving. We would listen to each person's story and make no comments. We were to just hold the story and the image of the person who had died in our hearts.

The woman on my right said she would go first. She was in her late thirties and perfectly made up, with red fingernails and a red polka dot ribbon that held back her thick, chestnut-colored hair. She was chatty and extroverted.

"Hello. My name is Ms. Rojas," she spoke clearly and directly. "I've had so many deaths and losses that I don't know where to start. My husband died a year ago from an overdose. I was in here, so that was kind of hard," she smiled at all of us, and I smiled back at her.

"I guess the hardest thing is that I just lost my best friend on the outside. She was with her boyfriend, and they were fighting. He put a gun to her head, and then he just pulled the trigger," she paused and then sat up straight in her chair and continued.

"My kids won't speak to me since I'm in prison. They're all real mad at me, and won't answer my letters or nothin'. It's hard not knowing how they're doing in school. I guess that could count as a loss, too, couldn't it?" We said yes that could count.

"So I guess I don't know what to talk about. I guess I should talk about my friend who was killed. Her name was Deena. We were friends from the second grade in Catholic school. Then we had to go to public school in fifth grade because our parents couldn't afford the private school any more. We started getting a little wild in the sixth grade, smoking, and things like that. Then one day, I came home from school in the middle of the day, and my mom was in bed with the shades pulled down. She said Dad had left us, and he was living on the other side of town with another woman. He had another family, and he never came back to us, and I guess my mom never really got out of bed either."

"I was fourteen and the oldest of the kids. Mom told me I had to take over for the family. They came and repossessed all our furniture. Deena helped me get a job at the dime store. I dropped out of school and eventually we got all of our stuff back. I was so proud the day I made the layaway payments for the refrigerator. My friend Deena, she was always there to help me out, babysitting the little kids, things like that. She brought food over to my house when her grandmother would make something special. We were always really tight. Then we both got hooked up with guys who were in the life. They had money and our life got a lot better. We bought clothes and makeup just like other sixteen-year-olds. We had a lot of fun back then. I'm sad that Deena was killed, but I know that the Lord loves us, and she is with Jesus now."

I thanked Ms. Rojas, and then moved on to the next person in the circle. She had pale blue eyes, bad skin, and lanky blonde hair. I guessed her to be in her late thirties.

"My name is Ms. Wilson, and I can't talk about it." We said that was fine and moved on.

The next woman, in her late twenties, with a wiry build, evidence of time she had spent at the gym. Her round glasses and curly brown, Afro-styled hair seemed like a throwback to the seventies.

"My name is Ms. Field. I'm here because of my son, Jimmy. He died two days after Christmas, seven years ago. He was three months old. I was staying with my husband's people up in the hills in West Virginia," she spoke with a very soft, southern accent. "We'd gone there to show his folks the baby. They hadn't seen him yet. It was their first grandbaby boy. They was so happy to see him. They was nice folks. They lived up the holler in a little old house. They had three of their own kids still in the house, so they didn't really have room for the baby and me and my husband, Matt. We put the baby in the dining room, in a crib right up next to the table. Me and Matt, we slept on the couch in the living room. At night we left the Christmas tree lights on, and we could see 'em all bright and twinkly, as we went to sleep. It was cold that night, but it didn't snow. I remember that. It didn't snow. Matt, he was gettin' restless. He didn't really like staying up there too long. There wasn't really nothin' for him to do. He asked me if he could go down to town and drink with his buddies, and I told 'em sure, go ahead. Matt, he was always good like that, asking me if he could do things. Polite like his kinfolk," she told the story as if she were reading it from a book.

"I went to sleep with them Christmas lights on. I remember feeling happy that night as I went to sleep thinkin' we'd had a good first Christmas with Jimmy."

"I woke up to a terrible noise. I thought it was Matt coming home. Trying to wake up I saw three big firemen standing in front of me asking me where the baby was. I didn't know what they was talkin' about. I thought I was having a nightmare," she sighed and paused holding her hand over her mouth. We sat in silence waiting for her to go on.

"Then I heard my mother-in-law, Mamaw, she's crying something about the baby not breathing. I'm still thinkin' this is a bad dream; I'll wake up in a minute. But them firemen, they ran out of there with the baby in their arms. Then, Mamaw, she came over and took a hold of me and shook me hard, and started screaming at me that the baby was dead. I just stared at her, knowing I wasn't dreamin' no more. Jimmy was gone."

"They said it was Sudden Infant Death Syndrome. Mamaw said she went and checked on the baby, and he wasn't breathing. She tried to get him to breathing on her own, and then called the firemen. She didn't think of getting me. I reckon I'd a done the same, but still, I wish I'd held Jimmy before he was cold. They thought it was strange that I didn't mourn the baby. I didn't keen for the baby like they do up in the hills. Don't know why I didn't, really I don't. Never did cry. What's the use? Tears never came to me. It was like my insides was made of dead animals you see along the road. Before Jimmy died, I had me a good job up at the mill. Never missed a day of work. After Jimmy died, I could see Matt watchin' me, thinkin' it was my fault. Why didn't I wake up? Why didn't I check on Jimmy? Why was it Mamaw that discovered him and not me? I know he thought it. I thought it too. I started drinking then, and then doing other stuff. Lost my job. Matt, he couldn't put up with it no more. Told me to get straight or get out. I left in the middle of the night. Never took nothing. I didn't blame 'em. Heard he remarried a nice girl up his way."

We sat silently in the middle of the sadness of her story. I turned to hear the last woman speak.

She was around her mid-twenties with beautiful long, brown, auburn-colored hair, perfect delicate features and luminous large brown eyes that were constantly filled with tears.

"My name is Ms. Alvarez and I'm here because my case manager told me I had to come," she started out softly, staring at the floor. We could hardly hear her. She talked slowly and she seemed blurred, as if she were underwater.

"I can't get out of bed; I wish I could sleep my life away. I went over to psychology. They've given me a bunch of pills. They just make me sleepy, which I am thankful for."

We waited for her to go on, but she sat silently, staring vacantly into her lap. It seemed like time was slowly dripping through the room.

"I had four children. They were taken away from me because of the drugs. Three of them got put in one foster home, but they couldn't take the baby. She was ten months old and put in a different foster home. They wouldn't let me visit the children 'til I got cleaned up. I went north to a clinic. One of my, uh, sponsors paid for it," she paused. I glanced at Chaplain Gerber who sat still as a rock. She spoke with such sadness, with such a heavy heart, that it took all of the life out of the room.

"I had voluntarily checked myself into rehab," she started back again with a slow dirgelike rhythm. "I was halfway through the program. I was doing well. Everyone there was proud of me. I was beginning to understand some things that I hadn't understood before. One night I got a call. They said I had some visitors. I went down to the lobby, and my mom was there with a cop and a detective. My mom wouldn't look at me. I knew something bad had happened. She was white as a ghost, and she seemed out of it, knowing what I soon would find out." She sat back in her chair, and looked up at us for the first time.

"The cops told me my baby was dead. I didn't believe them. I was sure they'd made a mistake. They took me to the medical examiner to see and identify the baby. I still didn't believe the baby was dead. I looked through the glass at the baby and told the doctors to give the baby something to make her wake up. I pleaded with them. I was sure that the baby was just asleep. I begged the baby to wake up. I knew that if I could just hold the baby that she would wake up and it would be ok, but they wouldn't let me hold her. I begged and pleaded but they took me away. I left but was sure the baby just needed medicine. I became hysterical, crying, begging, and crying. Finally they gave me something that knocked me out." We sat silently, waiting for her to continue.

"My mother knew the baby was dead. She said that the foster father had beaten the baby to death. Her intestines were broken, and the baby was dead. Mom told me we had to plan the funeral service. At the funeral, when I saw the baby in the little box, then I knew that it was true, but still I don't think I accepted it. I went crazy. I still can't understand it. If God wanted to take her, I could accept that, but why did the baby have to suffer? The baby was a good baby. She didn't fuss. She had no sin. I wish I could have taken her place but I can't. How could God let the man beat my baby to death?"

The question hung in the air, unanswered.

"They asked me if I wanted the death penalty for the man, but I thought what good would that do? I left rehab and got back into the life. I was in a blur. One night my husband and me were driving across the bridge from Mexico back into Texas, and he said, "Baby, get out of the car and walk. I got stuff in the car and we're gonna get stopped." I started screaming at him, 'After all I've been through, how could you do this to me?' But what was the use?"

"I don't care about being here as long as they let me sleep. When I'm asleep," she continued in a type of trance, "I'm with the baby, floating up above the cemetery. She and I are wrapped in each other's arms. It is a beautiful night with stars in the sky. I have a deep blue blanket that she loved wrapped around both of us. It's the only time I'm happy, when I'm asleep, flying with the baby, and she is still alive."

We were out of time. Open movement had begun. I quickly thanked the women for coming and told them we would meet again in a week. After the room emptied, Chaplain Gerber came up to me.

"That's as hard as it's going to get," Chaplain Gerber said as the women started leaving the room. I shook my head unable to speak. "Are you all right? This is pretty heavy duty for your first class."

"I'm okay," I lied. I wanted to go into the bathroom and throw up, but I didn't.

Thoughts of privilege, class, and justice were running through my mind. Ms. Alvarez, like many of the women, had a public defender. Had she had the money for a decent attorney, they would probably have gotten her a reduced sentence, knowing that her baby was brutally beaten to death just four months before her arrest. I had always believed that our system was fair and just. Now I questioned the viability of justice in an unjust world.

What are my beliefs about this? If God is good all the time, where is God in this interaction? How could any good come from the beating of the baby? The man who killed the baby is now in prison for life. The baby's mother and father were in prison for five years for running drugs in from Mexico. The rest of the children were still in foster care away from their parents.

It was not my first attempt to wrestle with the question of theodicy, a branch of theology that tries to justify the belief in a good and all-powerful God in a world where evil appears to run rampant. The famous dilemma: is God able to prevent evil and will not, or is God willing to prevent evil and cannot? I had no idea.

Historically, my tendency had been to discover unintended good in the suffering. Such as, maybe the baby would have grown up to be a mass murder. But then, why did the baby have to be beaten to death? Maybe the baby had lived a previous life and this was her karma in this life. Even if this is true, it seems like a cold-hearted approach to suffering. I have wrestled with the question of theodicy since I was a child. I had always believed that people smarter than me could figure this out, and I would leave it at that. It now seemed vitally important for me to develop clarity about my belief if I were to continue this work, and not lose my mind, my heart, or my faith.

Many theologians talk about free will, that we are all created with a sense of choice. We can choose to act selfishly and suffer the consequences or we can act for the greater good. I believe that, but still it seems like some of us are left with choices that seem like no choice at all. How much choice did the baby have? Did the baby have to suffer because of the choices made by the mother? If so, where is a just God in that system? My time in prison pushed the reality of cruelty, human savagery, and evil into my face, and I was unable to turn away. The Buddhists say it is important to hold the knowledge of the beauty of a rose and ten thousand starving children in one mind. I have spent a lifetime acknowledging the rose, and now I had turned to face the reality of the starving and sometimes beaten to death children.

Besides questions of theodicy that were raised in the grief group, I also realized that I had been fooling myself about my own grief, not only had I not dealt with it, I hadn't even brought it up to the surface.

Chapter Four

ENLIGHTENMENT AND GREEN BEANS

Knowing others is wisdom, knowing yourself is enlightenment. —Lao Tsu

---

"It's cancer," my mother said weakly into the phone from my sister Diane's hospital room. I felt the floor start to slide beneath my feet. I was standing in the kitchen in my home in Irvine, California, holding on to the phone for dear life. I had felt sure that Diane's tumor would have been benign. A few months before, doctors had diagnosed me with a uterine fibroid that turned out to be benign and required surgery and a short recovery period. A few months later, Diane received a similar diagnosis. She and I had joked about our dual surgeries and whether we should get tummy tucks together. That anxious feeling, a constant resident in my stomach, now spread throughout my body. I was fine and healthy, but my sister had stage IV ovarian cancer. Why was I ok? Why wasn't she? Ovarian cancer killed my mother's sister and my father's mother, as well. The curtain of a privileged reality, and a belief that my sisters and I were protected from harm from the external world, was torn asunder, never to be mended.

Over the years, Diane and I had become close friends. She got over the fact that I wasn't five years old when I was born, and I no longer tried to convert her. She protected me as much as she could from my mother's temper. She fought for me to be able to go to Europe to school, and for my parents to buy me a car when I graduated from college. As we both grew older, Diane had become the perfect older sister, protective, funny, and caring. We talked several times a week and were current with each other's lives. In a strange way, as I became more separated from my mother, Diane remained locked in a power struggle with her. Although Diane moved out of the house after my parents sold it, I realize now Diane never really left home. After Sarah and I left the house, Diane stayed very connected to my parents, acting once again as the only child. She was always fighting with my mother, always wanting our mother to be like other mothers. I gave up on that idea a long time ago.

Diane had moved to Tennessee to run my father's tool and die business after our parents relocated. She was the larger than life Auntie Mame character, who loved life. Diane loved eating, drinking, and having fun. She particularly loved living in Tennessee and running my dad's business and generally wrecking havoc in my mother's life. I thought she was nuts. I moved to California, and loved living there. She thought I was nuts. The two things we agreed on was that we loved one another and we both thought our mother was nuts.

Sarah had moved to New Jersey, married, had a little girl, divorced, and stayed in New Jersey. Although many miles separated us, we stayed connected and involved in each other's lives through regular visits and weekly phone calls.

I had spent my twenties and thirties trying to grow up. In 1966, when I was twenty years old, Time magazine ran a front page that asked the question, "Is God Dead?" The article referenced William Hamilton, a theologian from a seminary in upper New York State. He postulated that the concept of God had become irrelevant in today's secular society. He believed that people should care for one another without the idea of a reward in heaven. Although he didn't say church was unnecessary, I inferred this from his comments about God, and felt vindicated in my newfound agnosticism. The article also spoke to my twenty-year-old desire for freedom from the tight constraints of evangelical Christianity. I stopped going to church, stopped praying, and stopped being interested in the meaning of life, purpose, or the question of evil. I surrounded myself with people who wanted to have fun, and there is nothing like country club southern people if you want to learn how to party, eat, drink, and be merry.

I returned to Tennessee to marry my college sweetheart. I tried and discarded different roles as easily as I tried on and rejected new coats, I later told my first therapist. I started out as a southern Junior League housewife, a role that exposed the soft power of a well-bred southern woman. My rebellion against this role led me to the role of a sexually liberated rebellious woman, which led me to my first divorce. I tried being a teacher of French and English in Appalachia, during which time I married and divorced again. Nothing filled the internal dread and foreboding that ate at me like termites scuttling through the base of my soul. Eventually, like many of the disaffected young people of my generation, I escaped to California. And there, for the first time, other than Italy, I found myself at peace with my surroundings and the geographical distance from my mother.

While living in southern California in 1984, I received the news of Diane's cancer diagnosis. This made me decide to try God again. I raised my face to the sky and prayed from the spirit of my nine-year-old self, making a pact that if God saved Diane, I would return to the church, become a good Christian, and try my best to be the good girl I was meant to be. My feeble bargains met with infinite silence.

My mother's attitude regarding Diane's illness was seen through her lens of narcissism. Why did she have to have a daughter with cancer? Diane, tired of my mother's self-absorption and proselytizing, banished Mother from her sickbed, and ultimately died without reconciling with her. Diane said she had spent a lifetime trying to gain my mother's approval and love, and she said now she was sick, she would not waste one minute of her energy on this futile pursuit. It was an attitude I understood, but it saddened me nonetheless. My mother, however, was indifferent to her banishment and said "That was Diane for you."

My younger sister Sarah took Diane into her home so Diane could more easily commute to Sloan Kettering in New York City, for her treatment. Diane lived with Sarah for nine months. My dad left his work in Tennessee and went up to stay with Sarah to see if he could help. My mother stayed in Tennessee, and I was working and did not leave California. I felt furious at my mother for not going to the hospital to be with Diane, even though Diane didn't want Mother near her. I now realize that my anger was misplaced anger at myself that I didn't quit my job and go to the hospital, either. The work of caretaking fell squarely on the shoulders of my sister Sarah and my dad.

Diane and I talked on the phone every day. She would tell me funny stories about the hospital and the nurses. We didn't talk about her illness. We didn't talk about her pain. We didn't talk about her fears. We didn't talk about her regrets. Most of all, we didn't talk about her impending death. One day, she called and said that the doctors suggested she have her spinal cord cut as a way to deal with the pain she was having. She didn't want to do it, because once she got better, she wanted to get pregnant and she didn't want to be in a wheelchair. Even though she was forty-five years old and in stage IV of ovarian cancer, I told her I agreed with her. She did not have the surgery.

Sarah and I coped with Diane's illness by learning everything we could about ovarian cancer, and what we learned was not good. Ovarian cancer presents with very vague symptoms. It is more common in women over 55 and women who have never had children. Diane, like many women with ovarian cancer, had pain caused by a tumor that had grown next to her spine. By this time, the cancer had metastasized and there was no known cure. In spite of these medical facts, the family pushed on in a belief that she would get well. Diane, my strong warrior sister and protector, never accepted that she was going to die, and so Sarah, Dad, and I never accepted it either. My mother, ever the realist, told us all that it was hopeless and that Diane would die just as her own sister had died.

I made one trip to New York City to see Diane, and it was one of the hardest days of my life. Her hair, which she had always kept a bright red orange, had all fallen out and had come back in a shocking white. She was in constant pain, but, as always, tried to put on a good face for me. The day I visited she was taken to radiation and then chemo. I will never forget the fear on her face as they put her on a gurney and wheeled her out of the room. They were throwing everything they could at the cancer, hoping to slow down its progress. She was a valiant fighter who did not give up even at the end.

One night, Diane called me in the middle of the night. I remember looking at the clock and noting that was 1:15 am. She asked me to tell her about my day. Nothing particular had happened that day, so I didn't really know what to say. I was sleepy and almost told her I would call her back in the morning, but there was something about her voice that made me stay on the line. I told her about my job, my friends, and the neighborhood I lived in. I told her silly stories about my dogs, my boss, anything I could think of. I talked on for over two hours. I kept thinking she had fallen asleep on me, but then she would pipe up and tell me she was there, and she wanted to remember my life. Finally, she said that she needed to go to sleep. It was the last time I talked to her. My sister died on June 6, 1985, nine months after her initial diagnosis.

I don't remember who called to tell me that Diane had died, maybe my mother, maybe my sister. I know it wasn't my dad. His grief was inconsolable, leaving him incapable of talking on the phone. Diane had always been very close to my dad. She drove into work with him when we lived in Michigan, and then she went to work for my dad after he moved his business to Knoxville. She had an adult/adult relation with him, something I was never able to achieve. Dad and Diane had a similar sense of humor and they adored one another. My sister Sarah later said that she and Dad had bonded on trying to get Diane well and they were bonded in their failure once she died.

Once again, I was standing on the rim of the family, not wanting to go into the emotional and physical pain and fear. Every morning, I woke with a terrible knot in my stomach wondering what was wrong, and then I would remember it was Diane, the strong one who had not made it. I pushed my grief into a little box and put a wall back up to protect myself from the pain of my grief.

On the day of Diane's funeral, I unexpectedly had a vision of her in the afterlife. This had never happened to me before, although it had happened to my mother and her mother. Actually, Diane appeared to Sarah first, but it scared the heck out of her, and she told Diane's spirit to go away. When Diane appeared to me, for some reason I wasn't afraid. She didn't appear like a ghost or an apparition; instead she was inside my head and showing me where she was. Diane showed me a brilliant colorful picture of the universe where everything was beautiful and everything was connected. Years later, Steve Jobs' last words on his deathbed were reported to be, "Oh wow, oh wow, oh wow." This is how I felt at the vision that Diane unfolded to me. It showed a beauty beyond any beauty I had ever seen. Diane's voice reassured me that she was very busy but doing fine. She gave me some final instructions for friends and then, she said she would see me in the basement, whatever that meant, and she disappeared. I felt captivated by the power of the vision. I wanted to hold it in my mind and hands forever, but it faded a little with each passing day.

Diane's connection to me after her death did not fit into my agnostic, atheistic framework. I couldn't make any logical sense of it. She was one of the least religious people I knew. She had a total disdain for organized religion and never went to church again once she could make that choice. How was it that she was able to make a vision like this happen? Why was she busy? What was she doing? I later learned about a church called the Universalist, that described the world in terms that I experienced during this vision, but at the time, I had no knowledge of such a thing.

I had two more visitations from Diane that next year. The first was at a restaurant, The Hobbit, an old Victorian house in Orange County that had been converted to a restaurant. Very unusual for most houses in California, it had a basement that was used as a wine cellar. I was with a group having wine and cheese, and I split off from the group, rounded a floor to ceiling rack of wine bottles and came upon my sister Diane. She appeared like a hologram, as if I could put my hand through her. Seeing her there shocked me speechless. In life she had been very overweight, even at the end of the cancer. In this incarnation, she was thin, dressed in a long, purple and silver evening dress. I couldn't think what to say to her except to remark about how beautiful she was. She responded, "Your way of seeing is not my way of being," and then she disappeared.

The last time I experienced her, I was driving on the 405 freeway in Southern California, on a section of the highway that had about five lanes, and I was in the second to the left lane. It was dark, and I was tired, driving home from my job as head of Human Resources at a small computer company. Driving a red 1986 Thunderbird, and not really paying attention to the road around me, I was thinking about a problem employee I had at work, and suddenly out of nowhere, I felt Diane's arm reach across me. It startled me, and I instinctively put on the brakes. Just at that moment, the car driving to the left of me had a blowout and went sideways across five lanes of traffic, luckily missing everyone on the road. Had I not put on my brakes, the driver would have certainly crashed into me, and I most certainly would have crashed into others. It was the last time I had a connection with Diane.

I found an Irish, Jesuit therapist with whom I shared my vision of Diane. He told me not to share it with others, because if I did, the visions impact would diminish both in my heart and in my spirit. We discussed the reality of these visions, and he counseled me not to try to make sense of it with my logic, as this did not come from a logical place. As you can imagine, this was not so easy for me. I also told him that my father was not adjusting to Diane's death as well as my mother, sister, and I were. My father cried every day, and he wanted to talk about Diane every time we were together. Each time her name was mentioned, it was like a knife in my gut, and I turned away from my father's pain when he spoke. I was sure that this torturing grief was not healthy. How could my father be cured, I wanted to know, and oh, by the way, why did I keep getting divorced when no one else in my family did? I still remember the perplexed look on my therapist's face as he asked, "Has it occurred to you that your father is the only normal one who is expressing his grief? Have you ever wondered why you get married rather than why you get divorced?"

"No," I responded to both questions, and quit therapy. Clearly, this was not my path to spiritual enlightenment.

Believing that I had finally found "the one," and this time I was actually right, I married for a third time and moved with my new husband, Gary, to Northern California. I worked in human resources for Apple Computer, where I found coming from a dysfunctional family was a definite career advantage. I was swept into the Apple culture of "meritocracy" and technology—a materialistic world where perfect design became the soul of the machine. It was the early nineties, Steve Jobs had left, and we had new leadership. They spent money freely and made money just as quickly. There were dogs at work, children in the child care center, and people who were paid to think, regardless of their position. Initially, I found the conversations exhilarating, like sophomore year in college. I was one of the oldest people around, and eventually the baby geniuses began to be more tiring than amusing.

I left Apple to become head of human resources at an Apple IBM spin-off called Taligent. The CEO who began the company resigned, and a new CEO from IBM took his place. His name was Dick Guarino, and he and I connected in our worldview as well as business view. Dick was about 5'10" tall, with a loose body that still seemed to have room for the one hundred pounds he had lost over the years. He was bald, with a swirl of white hair at the base of his head. His most distinguishing characteristic was his left eye, which was rounder and bigger than his right eye. This asymmetry was caused by a stroke that Dick had had years earlier. He had a wicked sense of humor, and when he laughed half of his face lit up and the other half looked like it really wanted to laugh but couldn't. Dick was from Connecticut, and was constantly amused at the Apple culture and the culture of Silicon Valley, with people who brought their dogs to work, refused to wear shoes, and generally acted outlandish. I regaled him with my stories of trying to fit proper IBM and the free-spirited Apple together. He became not only a boss but also a dear friend.

One Friday, he stopped into my office and said that he wanted me to do him a favor. I said sure, what is it? He asked me to accompany him in my car as he ran along the road. He had been having some pains and wasn't sure if it were muscular or chest pains. I tried to persuade him to go to the hospital, but he said that he was going to run either with me or without me. I slowly followed him for a while, and he eventually got in the car. He said that he would need to make a doctor's appointment for Monday and then we went out to dinner. During the dinner he told me about his mother, and how he loved her. He talked about his uncles, told me stories about both of his daughters and the rest of his large Italian family. We had a very happy dinner. We ate at a small Japanese restaurant and he told me he had become a vegan because of his heart problems. I had that sense of genuine connection to someone that I not only respected but also truly loved as a human being. The next day, Dick's two daughters flew out from Connecticut, and they went into San Francisco to see "Phantom of the Opera." The girls flew home Sunday morning, and Sunday afternoon Dick once again went out jogging on one of the trails in Los Gatos. Sunday evening I got a call that Dick had collapsed on the jogging trail and died instantly. There was an EMT also jogging on the trail at the time, and he performed immediate CPR, but it was futile. Dick's last words were, "Wait a minute," as he went down on one knee and died.

Dick's death was another emotional tidal wave that swept through my life. He was 48, nearly the same age as I was. I had the responsibility of helping our company deal with the loss of a new but well liked leader, working through the details of the funerals on the East and West coast. When I went back East to Dick's funeral, I met all of the people that he had described that Thursday night at dinner, and with each I was able to recount a special vignette that he had shared with me about them.

Dick's death caused me once again to wrestle with my metaphysical questions. Why was I here? Is there really an entity that we refer to as God? How much of religion is a myth, and how much is real? Does any of this matter? Should we just live a life of pleasure and accumulation? That seemed to be the meaning that everyone in Silicon Valley was pursuing. It seemed like we were all playing a big Monopoly game, and the person with the most toys won. The pressure to do more, faster, more efficiently, more, more, more, left little time for contemplation or introspection. The toys were fun, the competition was exhilarating, and the money brought a true sense of freedom and safety, but somehow there was an emptiness about it that seemed only to be filled by new things or people. In this perfectly staged life people still got sick, suffered and died. Or worse, they died without being sick first, or even worse they got old and lingered into decrepitude. Was my family right that the only way to face the reality of our human situation was to stay in denial until the end?

My husband Gary and I joined the Unity church of Palo Alto. At a service one evening, I felt God's presence, and I realized that my faith had been restored somehow, through the death of my sister and Dick. This realization came as somewhat of a shock. I no longer was an atheist or an agnostic. I knew I had faith in something; I just didn't know what it was. Where did I go from here? Was there a way I could find a teacher who would help me in my attempt to understand the universe and my place in it?

My sorrow about Dick's death was superimposed on my unresolved grief and sense of guilt about my older sister's death. Death brings back memories of other deaths. Why didn't I go back and see my sister more often? Why was I alive and she was not? Were the visions I had of Diane real, or just an overly active imagination? Was it a coincidence that Dick had reviewed his life with me two days before he died, or was it some unknown force at work? What did these events mean to my faith if they were real, and what did they mean to my sanity if they weren't? I decided I needed help, so I turned to my current therapist.

"I need a spiritual teacher," I said to Sondra, my therapist. She sat quietly and smiled at me. I continued, "I think you know who it is that I should work with." Sondra squirmed in her seat.

"Why would you think that?" she asked in her therapist tone of voice.

"Okay Sondra, I'm not getting any younger and I need to figure this out before I croak. God knows how much time I have. You're a transpersonal psychologist; I know you have someone you can refer me to."

She sighed, moved around in her chair and said, "Susan, I don't know who it is. I think this is your struggle, as I told you."

I tried one of her techniques and sat in stony silence looking at her.

"Okay," she finally responded. "The only name that is coming to me is Joan Halifax. I don't know why that name is here, but if you are interested, you should check her out and try to figure this out for yourself."

I was relieved. I had a name. I was now truly on my way to some answers. Now I only had to find this woman and get her to answer my questions. How hard could that be?

After doing a little research, I found out that Joan Halifax was a Buddhist, of all things, who taught several different courses. Joan ran a Zen center called Upaya in Santa Fe. I called the center to find out what classes were available in the near future, hoping I might start with some easy meditation class. They had an opening for a four-day course on "Being with Dying and the Encounter with Death." Ugh. I couldn't even sit through a one-hour course on grief. The subject gave me the creeps. I asked what other classes she taught—none that year. I paused, took a deep breath, and told them I wanted to register. I was now on my way to what I later referred to as Buddhist Boot Camp.

A week later, they sent me a brochure. It was beautifully designed; black, three-page foldout with a gold half circle artistically painted on the front, and seemed to present a retreat that was both elegant and welcoming. The text described the session as "an endeavor to inspire a gentle revolution in our relationship to dying and living." This didn't sound too bad. I had never known a Buddhist but I had an image of a warm earth mother, like the people who hung out at the spa where I got massages. Included in the price of the retreat were meals, vegetarian, which I guessed I could live with, and accommodations at the center. I found out this meant sharing a space with four other women. I decided to stay at a nearby bed and breakfast at night and at Upaya during the day. In retrospect, it would have been helpful had I known there are many types of Buddhism, and Zen Buddhists are not particularly known for a nurturing approach.

Santa Fe is a town that belongs in another country. The central plaza anchors the heart of the city. Outside of the Palace of the Governors, the Native American vendors were selling their wares on the sidewalk; small dress shops, candy stores, and restaurants lined the other side of the plaza. A large oak tree provided shade, and a circular, multi-tiered fountain added a cooling sound against the heat of the day. This is a city that beckons you to slow down—enjoy the pace, the food, the art galleries, and the different cultures. It is a city with soul. I could not believe my search for meaning had led me to this Catholic city and to a Buddhist retreat. This was as far away from my Baptist roots as I could imagine. I felt incredulous that I had actually made it here.

The bed and breakfast I chose had a wine and cheese event every evening around 6:00. I met the other patrons, all couples in their mid-thirties. They were curious as to why I was going on a four-day retreat on death and dying. They had all planned days of walking tours or art galleries, and massages at a local spa. When I went to my room that night, I asked myself the same question. What was I doing here? What was I really searching for? Whatever it was, how was I supposed to find it at a Buddhist retreat center in a Catholic city?

That night, I had a dream that I remember as vividly now as when I had it. In my dream, I was in Santa Fe and an older male with a long white beard began talking to me. He showed me how you could put your hand through a mirror into another reality. He encouraged me to push through the glass in the mirror, and to walk through the mirror. In my dream, I felt terrified and put only my hand through as I felt the mirror part like water. The experience scared me. My breathing became so heavy and my heart started beating so hard that I woke myself up. I sat up in bed and checked out my room, noting the mirror on the wall across from me. The supernatural has always scared me, and I have never wanted to dabble in the "black arts" as they were called back then. Was Buddhism a brush with the supernatural? Was I going to go into another dimension? I sincerely hoped not!

There was nothing spooky about Upaya, thank heavens. It is beautiful, tranquil, and harmonious in every way. The buildings, made in a typical adobe style, hug the earth and blend in with the landscape. The vigas, or wooden beams, protruded from the walls and created a shaded walkway in front of some on the buildings. Upaya is a compound of maybe four or five outbuildings connected by gravel paths bordered by desert plants. What I saw made me feel very optimistic. It appeared like a well-designed country inn I might have chosen to stay in had I been on vacation. I walked up the winding gravel path and opened one of the large wooden doors that led into the main house. There was no one around, but I found an envelope with my name on it sitting on the Asian style desk in the entryway. I took the envelope, sat down on one of the couches, and opened it to see what awaited me.

To put this Buddhist retreat center in context, you need to know there are two main schools of Buddhism: Theravada and Mahayana. Zen Buddhism is a school of Mahayana, which started in China then migrated to Viet Nam, Korea, and Japan. The Zen Buddhists are known as tough taskmasters. To the question "why do we meditate?" the Zen answer is "because your Master told you to." I was mercifully unaware of this as I picked up my ten pages of instruction. There were many questions I had about the material, but this was a silent retreat. This meant, no talking; I mean no chit chatting, no how are you, gosh this is really hard, where are you from, why are you here, nothing, nada, no talking. Have I mentioned that I am an extrovert who does not know what I think until words come out of my mouth?

I noticed a group of people lining up on an outside path, and I silently joined the line. We walked together down another gravel path that led to a large, upraised, white, square monument called a "stupa." I later learned that the stupa held the relics or partial bones of one of the revered monks from the tradition of their community. We walked around the stupa three times, always in a clockwise movement, just as I had read. It felt like I had joined a silent group of zombies from Night of the Living Dead. Thank goodness the people in front of me seemed to know what to do, as I was stressing out thinking exactly which way was clockwise and which way was counterclockwise. Didn't it depend where I entered the clock?

Following others, I entered the Zendo. According to my instruction sheets the Zendo is the heart of the center. It is used for talks, services, and ceremonies, as well as for "zazen" or seated meditation. This was my first time doing sitting meditation, and I had paid particular attention to this part of the instructions. The first step after entering the Zendo was to bow toward the altar. Here was my first problem. Baptists were taught that "bowing to graven images" was a straight path to hell. I was positive the golden statue of Tara, the goddess of compassion, placed at the front of the Zendo would be considered a real "graven image" by anybody's standards, not just the Baptists. I took a deep breath and bowed as instructed, "Fingers together, straight with the tips of the fingers about a fist's distance from the nose." Got it. Do not cross through the middle of the aisle. Do not cross directly in front of the altar. Always turn clockwise. Put your "zafu" cushion on your "zabuton" black mat and bow to your cushion, bow to the person across from you. Bow to the person to the right of you, bow to the person to the left of you. Then sit on your cushion cross-legged and swivel around and face the blank white wall with eyes half open.

Fortunately for me, I didn't know that I would be sitting on this dear old zafu cushion for three hours. We were instructed that the point of the sitting meditation practice was to stabilize the mind. I certainly knew that my mind needed stabilizing, so I tried to concentrate and do as Joan instructed. "Bring your attention to your breath. Count your exhalations from one to ten. If you lose your way in a thought, feeling, or sensation, return to one and begin again. Easy does it." I must confess this was impossible. Easy does it? I was a wreck. How many things went wrong? Let me count the ways. First of all, I was facing a white wall, nothing of interest to look at, which of course was the point. Next, I was bored out of my mind, which was the other point. There was no way to escape, so I had to sit with my boredom and see what happened. What happened was something Buddhists call "monkey mind," and I had at least twelve tribes of monkeys chattering constantly inside my head with admonitions, questions, fears, and distractions.

I would start as instructed: breathe in, breathe out, one. Breathe in and breathe out, two, then I got lost in some thought. I couldn't get past two so I started to count as fast as I could from one to ten, which was vaguely satisfying, but I was afraid I was going to hyperventilate and fall off my cushion. I started again at one, breathing in and out; two, breathing in and out, and I began to wonder what we would have for dinner. Back to one. I tried to go slowly, make a game of it, but before I knew it, I was planning my next vacation, and couldn't remember what number I was on—back to one. My limbs were tingling, should I move my legs or leave them be? Back to one. My body itched in places I didn't even know existed. Should I scratch them or leave them be? Back to one. In order to spare the reader from the same tedium I experienced, I will tell you that one time I got to four but that was with a concentration I could only muster once. I found that it was easy to let my mind wander where it wanted to go. I learned that, mainly, my mind likes to plan dinner parties and vacations.

Just when I was enjoying a future, particularly jovial, dinner party, Joan would drone out, "Focus on your breathing, breathe in and breathe out with a smile." Back to one.

After three hours, a gong sounded and I almost fell off my zafu with relief. Now the hard part. I had to stand up. My left leg buckled. I had no feeling from the tip of my toes to the top of my thighs. They should use this as a way to anesthetize people. The woman next to me caught me as I was about to topple over into the row in front of us. I could just imagine twenty-five Buddhists going down like bowling pins. We then did the bowing thing again, first to our cushions, one another, the Tara statue at the front, and then we shuffled out of the Zendo. I had survived the first morning.

That afternoon, we did a meditation where we paired up and stared deeply into each other's eyes to see if we could find the Buddha in one another. I was paired with a well-to-do, middle-aged aristocrat from Mexico. I knew she was an aristocrat because she told me so. She had beautiful posture, luxuriant brown hair, brown eyes, tasteful silver jewelry, and very pale white skin. She told me it was very important that I find the Buddha in her. I was immediately on duty.

Now, dear reader, take a leap of faith with me and know that as far as I know I had not been slipped a psychotropic drug, and the following really did happen. We sat together, slowly breathing in and breathing out. Our breath became synchronized and it felt as if I were one with her. I was in a state of deep relaxation, and I gazed deeply into her large brown eyes, and there I saw, ever so briefly, a fleeting image of…a blonde woman with pigtails. It was as if a hologram was flashed across her eyes. I was startled and said something intelligent like "Whoa!" She of course asked "Did you see the Buddha?" and I said "No but…"she interrupted me and commanded me to keep looking. I took another deep breath and again stared deeply into her eyes, breathing in and out, concentrating, and then in another flash I saw a soldier dressed in a uniform from the Civil War. "Whoa," I said again. Again, she asked, "Did you see the Buddha?" I said, "No but I saw…" She interrupted me once again and said, "I don't care what you are seeing; just keep searching for the Buddha." By this time I was completely rattled. I apologized to her and told her I was new at this and I was stricken with monkey mind. "Oh, no," she lamented, "why did I get stuck with you? This is life and death for me and I'm stuck here with a novice. Do you know what this means to me?"

"No," I honestly replied.

"Well," she said, "like everyone else here I have been diagnosed with a terminal disease." Ok let's stop right there. This was clearly news to me. I thought the retreat was about people who thought about death and dying but weren't actually dying in that moment. Good grief. I could not believe I was here. I looked around at the group with new eyes and realized many of them did indeed appear sickly. I suddenly wasn't feeling so great myself.

She continued, unaware of my latest realization. "I have to find someone who can see the Buddha in me." I was speechless.

I thought she was going to have a total breakdown right there in front of the smiling Buddha statue. "I'm sorry I am so desperate seeming to you, but two years ago, I literally died on the operating room table. When I died, I went to hell and then they revived me."

"You went to hell? Are you sure? Maybe it was a bad chemical reaction." I asked in what seemed like a calm voice. Inside I was asking, what about the blinding light? What about the Hallmark music with flowers and dogs and angels? She glared at me and I think would have taken a stick to me had there been one available. Instead she said, in what I thought was a rather huffy tone of voice, "I am quite certain it was hell. There were demons and devils chasing me." I had to admit this didn't sound like a Hallmark card situation. "Anyway," she continued, "I have been on a spiritual quest ever since. I have spent tens of thousands of dollars on my search. It has led me to do past life regressions, which is how I know you saw someone. Was it the general, the farmer, or the blonde?"

"It was the blonde," I admitted meekly.

"I am not interested in those past characters. So what if I were someone else in another lifetime? How does that help me now? I have done lucid dreaming, hypnosis, meditation. I need to find the Buddha in myself. They tell me I have three months to live, and no offense, but I don't think I can spend any more of my time with you."

"No offense taken" I replied. Then I asked, offhandedly, "Oh, did you see the Buddha in me?"

"No," she said, "All I saw was a well of deep sadness."

She got up, bowed to me, and rotated to the next person. In all my time working with people, she was the only person who ever shared a "going to hell" experience. I wondered if she might be better served spending her remaining time focusing on others, but I decided she probably didn't want to hear it. As far as her past lives and the images I saw, who knew? I was beginning to wonder about the tea they served.

We had a break and then continued with another meditation called a Tonglen meditation. The instruction was to breathe in and then allow all of our negative thinking, such as greed, anger, fear, attachment, and confusion to come to the surface, and then breathe out compassion. We did this several times and then we were to think of someone we loved, and let all of their negative thinking rise to the surface and then breathe out compassion. Next, we brought to mind someone we felt neutral about, and then someone we disliked, and then we thought about the entire world. It was a very holy feeling all of this thinking about the negative feelings and converting them to compassion. I felt like I did when I was baptized at twelve years old. I remember walking into the baptismal font in the front of the church, being lowered under the water by the pastor, and then coming up out of the water. I felt pure and blessed. I had the same feeling now as I tried to stay in the moment with the feeling.

We ended the session with a purification meditation. In this meditation, we visualized the world's suffering as black smoke that entered into our heart center. Joan said we needed to let go of the black smoke quickly or it could increase our own suffering. We then breathed out compassion for the rest of the world and for ourselves. There was something about that black smoke being in my heart center that totally freaked me out. I pictured black fumes entering and slowly constricting around my heart and lungs. When I felt the smoke hot and thick, I blew it out with as much force as I could muster. I continued blowing out as hard as I could, and realized I sounded like a woman trained to do breathing in labor, and I was in the last stages. I opened my eyes and noticed my new partner was staring at me with concern.

"Susan, are you all right?" she asked. I was embarrassed to be in such a state, and said nothing.

"I have liver problems," she said, "but I think I'll be okay. The treatment is really difficult, but they said it would give me three more years."

"I'm sorry." I replied not knowing what else to say. Sadness swept over me. I guess I did have a deep well of sadness in me, just as my last partner said.

"It's the way it is," she continued. "I live with it. Anyway, how did you do in the last meditation? It seemed like your breathing was really heavy. I was worried about you."

"I was worried I might get lung cancer with all of that black smoke going through my lungs and into my heart."

She put her hand on my leg in a gesture of reassurance. "It is just visualization. Nothing is actually happening. I don't think we are supposed to take it so literally."

"Oh. What about the Buddha? Were we supposed to see an actual sitting Buddha in the other person's eyes?"

She smiled and said, "I never have. I search for a feeling, a sense of the Buddha. Did you see an actual Buddha?"

"No," I said and smiled. The session was over.

Several thoughts came to me. One, my mother always told me I was too literal and susceptible to others. I guess she was right. Did this have something to do with my search for enlightenment? I couldn't figure it out. Was I supposed to have an actual enlightenment, or a metaphor for enlightenment? If so, how was I going to know what the metaphor was and what it meant? I hate metaphors.

The next day, we did a walking meditation. If I thought people were like zombies before, I was sure I was turning into one now. We were supposed to focus on our feet and mindfully walk. As far as I could tell, you walked around slowly with the cadence of a spaced-out Frankenstein monster. I did not find enlightenment. I did, however, find a remarkable stone, or more like a rock. Made of pink granite, it fit perfectly in my right hand. With this rock in my hand, I could bop on the head any of those demons that came after me.

Later in the afternoon, I returned to the B&B feeling hungry and discouraged. I had skipped the tofu dinner and left after the walking meditation. The Mexican woman who cooked breakfast for the guests was at the B&B when I arrived. She could tell by my face that I wasn't happy and asked me what the matter was. I told her I felt discouraged because I didn't think I was learning what I was supposed to be learning. She asked, "What are you supposed to be learning?" I told her I was supposed to be learning how to be with dying people. In order to do that, I had to sit on a cushion for three hours facing a white wall and nothing happened, and then I was supposed to look into someone's eyes and find the Buddha but all I found was a soldier and a blonde. Then we were supposed to breathe in all of the suffering of the world and breathe out compassion, and I was afraid I was going to get lung cancer. Finally, I told her that we were not allowed to eat meat or have spices in our food or drink any alcohol. Apparently, this was the living end for her. She stared at me, started wringing her hands, and then started mumbling in Spanish, something about the day of the dead and crazy Americans. She told me to follow her into the kitchen where she fixed me a fantastic dinner with meat, spices, and a glass of wine. She said maybe I should go shopping tomorrow like the other guests. It was a tempting thought.

In my sleep that night the old man with the long white beard showed up again in my dream to talk to me. This time we were walking in a garden. We approached a long row of green bean plants and he stopped and told me to examine the plant.

"What do you see?" he asked me.

"Green beans," I said. They looked like green bean plants I had seen in my mother's garden. The plants were trained onto small wooden stakes and the beans seemed ready for picking. They hung heavy on each of the plants.

"Do you see how each green bean is separate but each is part of the plant?" he asked me.

"Yes. So what?" I asked in the usual pissed-off tone of voice I use when talking to the enigmatic ones.

"Well," he continued patiently, "this is just like you."

"I'm like a green bean?"

"Yes. You are like a green bean."

I woke up, and wondered if this meant I was supposed to be a vegetarian.

The next morning I did not go shopping. I returned to the Sangha, willing to give it one more try. We started with a two-hour meditation, which was much easier because I found a chair to sit in. It was the same instruction, to count from one to ten and follow our breath. I failed again; couldn't make it past four and was not easy on myself. I wondered why I was really here. Maybe this whole thing was just a stupid waste of time. Why would any normal person subject himself or herself to this when they could be in beautiful art museums and galleries? Also, what did any of this have to do with dying people? I didn't get it. Joan continued to say, "Be easy with yourself." Just at the moment, I was whipping myself for my latest failure of concentration. After two hours it was over.

Later in the afternoon, Joan said that she was going to do a meditation that several people in the group had requested. She did not ordinarily do this meditation, and if anyone wanted to not attend that was okay. The meditation was called a Phowa meditation and is the practice of conscious dying. Okay, at least it seemed like we were on topic. This meditation is also described as a practice for the "transference of consciousness" or the practice of conscious dying. The mark of a successful Phowa practice is a small drop of blood emanating directly from the crown of the head. Before Joan started with the meditation, she said that she had people who "made their transition" during this meditation, and if that occurred to anyone in our group, we should know that we were in a safe place, and that dying was something we all came to. At this point, I was beyond scared. People actually died doing this meditation? If there is an emotion for "speechless" that would have been me. I did not do the exercise as Joan described, I didn't want a hole in my head, and I definitely didn't want to die in this room. Others around me, however, were very focused. The aristocratic Mexican woman was particularly interested in this exercise. As far as I know, there were no blood spots on people's scalps and no one died during this morning meditation.

Later in the day, we gathered for one final meditation. This was called the dying meditation. We weren't given any warnings about actually dying in this meditation, so I decided to go along with the instructions. Joan said it was a simulation exercise, which sounded safe enough. She told us to lie prone on our mats, face up with our feet facing the front of the Zendo. We did a relaxation exercise, where we let go of tension in every part of our body. If you have never done this type of meditation, it is beyond the relaxation of a really good massage. We were then told that we were on our deathbed. It was important for our mind to be calm and peaceful and alert. There is nothing else to do, nowhere else to go, everything is just to be and to let go.

Joan described all of the things that we would be leaving behind: our friends, our families, our possessions, our joys, and our sorrows. I was sad thinking of these things, during the meditation, but there was a sense of relief as well. She then went through all of our bodily functions, which corresponded to earth, water, fire, air, and space. Each of our senses eventually stops. The last of the senses to quit is our sense of hearing.

Then Joan said, "We all come to life on the in-breath and we all die on the out-breath. This is your last out-breath."

At that moment, I discovered what I had been searching for. For the first time in my life, I had no anxiety, I had no drive, I had no chattering voices inside, and I had only the sense of absolute connection and peace. Death was not the ultimate terror, but just another way of being. It was a state of peace, wholeness, and bliss all at the same time. There were times in my life when people would talk about infinity and it would create within me the deepest sense of agitation. How could we "do" something for infinity? It was at the end of this meditation that I understood how it would be in infinity. There is a deep sense of connection and loss of individual personality. It was a level of existence that I could not have imagined. When the chattering mind goes, the essence that is left is deep peace. Eventually, Joan called us back, but I did not want to get up. Everyone left the Zendo but me. I was in such a state of bliss I could not make myself rise up and leave. Eventually, Joan came for me and she helped me walk outside and sat me down on a bench. She walked away, and I sat there alone, in the sun, in the same state of perfect harmony. I noticed two pink finches had landed at my feet and they started pecking at each other. I remember thinking, oh, I am back on earth, and the feeling was gone.

The afternoon session closed with a discussion of what it takes to sit with dying people. The most important thing is to have a calm mind and an open heart that can hear the dying person's last stories. It is important to validate the life they have had here on this earth. I thought about Dick and the last meal we had together, and how he shared stories with me about each of his family members. Then I thought about my sister, and how I talked to her on the phone that night. She wanted me to share my life; she didn't want to share hers. In retrospect, I wish I would have had the courage to ask her about her life, her joys, her sorrows, if she had any regrets she wanted to talk about, but this conversation was not to be between us.

At the last session at Upaya, we closed with each person talking about their own illness, what they had learned, and what they would do with the learning. When it came my time to speak, I felt hesitant. I told them I was not Buddhist, and as far as I knew I was not dying any time soon, but I had a sister who died, and I wished we could have had a more conscious approach to her death, but we were all afraid. I made a commitment to take what I learned back to the Christian community, and apply it in the best way I could. My courage to make that commitment reinforced my faith, and my true spiritual journey began at that point.

Leaving Upaya, I flew from Santa Fe to Denver and then home. It was a very rough flight. Ordinarily, I am the original white-knuckle passenger when turbulence occurs. On this particular bumpy flight, however, my mind was calm. I felt at peace. I was not afraid. My courage had finally overcome my fears.

It didn't last.

Chapter Five

IDEOLOGIES IN CONFLICT

Ideologies separate us. Dreams and anguish bring us together.—Eugene Ionesco

---

"I don't want to deal with any radicals," I said to Lori as we sat together trying to decide how we were going to reach out to the inmates.

"Why's that?"

"I don't know. I don't have any patience for them. It is one thing to be a criminal, but it's something else to be like a normal person, and then voluntarily put yourself in prison for some ideal that's going nowhere. It seems really self-indulgent to me."

"Huh, I guess I don't quite see it that way." Lori was the best companion for me. Whereas I was a huge extrovert whose thinking was all done out loud, she was an introvert, who thought things through before speaking—a true novelty for me.

"Well, how do you see it?" I asked really curious about her opinion.

"I admire people who are willing to stand up for what they believe. They put themselves in harm's way for a belief that they hold. I'm not saying that I would do it, but I have to give them credit for walking their talk." I kept silent as I thought about that.

"I get what you're saying, but they still annoy me. Tell you what, if we get a radical, you can have her." Lori smiled her sweet smile at me.

"Radical or not, how are we going to reach the women? Lori asked. "Chaplain Becker thinks we ought to do ministry by walking around. What do you think?"

"Hanging out seems way too unstructured for me. It's like being a shepherd, and sitting down and waiting for the sheep to come. I think we should have programs like the Grief Group, although I have to say, I don't know if I can do a second one of those for a while. They really want us to do a Bible study group. Are you up for that?"

"Sure. But right now, I'm going to go out on the compound and sit for a while and see who comes by. It's open movement, so I'll let you know how it goes."

"Okay. I'll go talk to Chaplain Becker about the Bible study class.

I walked into the chaplain's office, and saw an inmate chatting with him.

"Hi Chaplain Pohl, I'm glad you dropped by. I'd like to introduce you to Ms. Heron. She's a member of the Plowshares group." I stared at him blankly.

"You know the Bible verse, Isaiah 2:4…they shall beat their swords into plowshares…"

I smiled, and said hello.

"Ms. Heron would like to talk to you about doing a Bible study group. Why don't you and she talk about how this might be done?"

"Sure. Come with me Ms. Heron," I said.

Once we were in the office with the door closed, Ms. Heron asked me if I knew who she was.

"No, I'm sorry. I don't know you," I truthfully replied.

"Have you ever heard of the Berrigan Brothers?"

"Yes. I remember they were activists in the sixties," I replied.

"Well, the Berrigan Brothers were more than activists. They were peace activists and nonviolent political activists."

"Were you part of their organization?" I asked, uncertain of what to say.

"I am a member of the Plowshares Movement. I'm here because I tried to disarm the Trident Submarine and Missile by pouring a vial of my blood on the missiles. As U.S. citizens we are responsible under the Nuremberg Principles for the actions of our government. We are called by Ezekiel to transform our hearts..." she continued, but I couldn't stay focused on her rhetoric. How do these things happen to me, I wondered. How many radicals are here, and how is it the one type of person I just said I didn't want to deal with is now sitting before me lecturing me on nonviolence and disarmament?

"...and so I was wondering if you would be willing to do a Bible study class with us?" I brought myself back from my wanderings and refocused on Ms. Heron.

"Yes. We can do that. We can start with the book of Mark, (I was studying that in the New Testament class and thought I could stay ahead of the study group by at least a chapter.)

"That's great," Ms. Heron said and smiled. "I look forward to it. The classes can't be longer than twenty minutes. That's about as long as I can take some of these drug heads. You know so many of them have lost a lot of cognitive functioning, and twenty minutes at a time is all I can take of being around them. I will be good to have some further conversations with you about nonviolence."

She thanked me and left.

Once the door closed, I felt my jaw loosen up. No wonder my teeth hurt, I needed to learn to stop clenching them. What was it I was supposed to learn from my encounter with the radical? Why was I presented with this woman right after I said I didn't want to work with someone like her? She was certainly passionate about her cause, but many people could be passionate about their cause and not go to jail. I guess I had never put anything on the line to the extent that I would be willing to go to jail for it. In thinking about the "common good" over the "Susan good," where did having the passion of one's convictions come in? This was too hard for me. No matter what, I would not willingly place myself in prison.

But wait; hadn't I just done that? What was the difference between my choice of prison and hers? Ugh.

The door opened and Lori walked in.

"Guess who I just met?" Lori asked with a look of amazement.

"A criminal, perhaps?" I said with a smile.

"Well, I guess. She was the most interesting woman. She was the backup singer in a really famous rock band until she got promoted to be a collector."

"You mean like someone who collects bills?"

"No. I mean like someone who carries a gun and serves as a "collector" if you don't pay for your drugs."

Our eyes widened as we thought through the ramification of this discovery.

"Well. At least she's in prison," I said. "I know, but Susan, the weird thing is she was really proud of being a collector because

she was the only woman in that position. She was going to tell me about some of her more interesting encounters, but I stopped her and asked her why she wanted to see a chaplain."

"What did she say?"

"She said she didn't necessarily want to see a chaplain. She just saw me sitting on the bench and thought she would stop by to chat. She left when the bell rang for the close of open movement. I have to tell you it was a little creepy talking to her."

"Yeah, no kidding. Well, while you were talking to Bonnie from Bonnie and Clyde, the radical I never wanted to meet came in to talk to me." Lori stared at me speechless, and started to laugh.

"Right. I'm never again saying I don't want to do something. Hear me God. I don't want to be like Jonah and wind up in the belly of a whale. Although, how much worse could a whale be than prison? Maybe the prison is a whale."

"So what was the radical like?" Lori responded, apparently not wanting to get into a theological discussion of Jonah.

"She seemed normal enough, until she started to talk about missiles and blood, and then I kind of zoned out."

Later in the day, I went to check in with Chaplain Becker. "Chaplain Pohl, I have another little situation I want to talk to you about. It concerns some complaints that we have had about the use of the chapel. It's mainly in the Latina community. Some of them are complaining that the Protestants are discriminating against the Catholic women. It is an interesting conflict. The older women here are generally Catholic, and they are very devoted to the Virgin of Guadalupe. Do you know anything about her?"

I shook my head no.

"She's a very beloved saint in Mexico, and they celebrate her day on December 12th. The Protestants, who are generally younger, are telling the Catholic women that they are worshipping an idol, and they are trying to prohibit the women from having a celebration on the 12th. I am concerned about this, and I want the Catholic women to be treated fairly. Think about it and let me know what approach you would take."

After he left I thought about my day. I had the radical to deal with, I had a Bible class to plan, Lori had just met a drug enforcer, and now we had Catholics and Protestants arguing in the chapel.

I went home that night totally exhausted, the stories of the women circulating in my head. The horrific stories from the women in the grief group hung in my heart, and my shoulders felt like a cemented knot. I knew that I had to do something to change my stress level. The next day, I had an emergency appointment with my dentist, sure that I had cracked a tooth. My jaw ached, and I couldn't sleep at night. My dentist assured me my teeth were fine, and then asked me if I were under any undue stress. I told her I was a new chaplain in a federal prison and I was carrying a full load of classes at school. The knowing look she gave me as I left the office told me I needed to make some changes, but I wasn't sure what to do.

One Monday, as I got ready to head to the prison, I couldn't find my chaplain badge with my name on it. It was nowhere. In a frenzy, I went through all my blouses, searched through the dirty clothes, and traced my steps in and out of the house. I begged my husband to help me find it; sure that it was in the house somewhere. After ten minutes, I tearfully concluded that it was nowhere to be found. I needed the badge to get past the stern lady at the front desk. As I drove to the prison, it felt as if my life were spinning out of control. I had no idea what I was doing at the prison, if I were helping or not, and I had no idea what I was doing in seminary. Maybe this whole sense of doing God's work was still the little girl going up during the altar call to make everyone happy, or maybe it was to make myself feel good about helping others, or maybe it was because I couldn't think of anything else to do. Strike that last thought, I could think of a lot of other things to do besides prison ministry. As I walked up to the front desk, the guard stopped me.

"Lose something?" I felt my stomach rise up into my throat. This could be the end of my internship right here. As my shoulders crept up around my ears, I nodded yes. She handed over my name badge.

"An inmate turned it in. She found it in the parking lot." I was so horrified, I didn't know what to say or do. I felt tears well up in my eyes.

"Don't worry," she said. "I didn't snitch on you. Just be careful with the clasp. It just came open, that's all. It came open and fell in the parking lot. You'll be okay." I turned away ashamed of my tears. It was the longest conversation she and I had ever had.

I later learned that during the time of my interactions with her, her husband was dying of cancer. I had no idea of the load she was carrying. Her act of kindness toward me that morning reminded me of why I went to seminary and why I was doing prison ministry. I realized that my call to service was to include everyone, not just the inmates, and not just the people who were nice to me. It was God's love that motivated my behavior when I was at my best. Later that day, I called my minister, Reverend Diana, and told her of the struggles I was having in the prison. She listened attentively to all of my stories, my feelings of responsibility, and my deep pockets of doubt.

After a few minutes, she told me that every day when I left the prison, she wanted me to wash my hands and say a silent prayer to God, turning the women back over to God and saying I had done the best that I could for that day. After I said my prayer, I was not to take the women back from God. It was a ritual that I followed religiously after that. Whenever I started worrying about the women, I would remember my prayer and then feel my shoulders and jaw relax. The prayer and ritual comforted me immeasurably.

The following week, Lori and I met to discuss our schedules and I told her about the problem in the chapel.

"Tell me again, what is the basic argument with the women? I mean there are Wiccans who use the chapel, so how can they have problems with other Christians who use the chapel?"

"That's a good point, Lori. The thing is that the Protestants call themselves Christians and they call the Catholics, Catholics."

"What?"

"It's true. I pointed out to one of the women that Catholic people were Christians also. She said 'no they aren't; they're Catholics.' I said that's correct they're Catholic Christians. She just stared at me and gave me "the look." The problem is that the Catholics also refer to themselves as Catholics and the Protestants as Christians. I think it is more than a question of semantics."

"Probably so, but what can we do about it?" Lori asked.

"I want to try an exercise that I have used when I was in business. You take a group of people in conflict, in this case hand-selected Catholics and Protestants and then pair them up, and ask them to share information."

"Like what?"

"In this case, I have three questions in mind: one, tell your faith story and how you came to know God. Two, what is the most difficult thing about your walk with God now? And, three: how does your faith sustain you in a place like this? What do you think?"

"I think it is a good thing to bring to the theological reflection group and get input from the others."

The group decided to go along with my suggestion, and we prescreened sixteen inmates suggested by the chaplains: eight Catholics and eight Protestants. I decided it was a good thing for the women to be interviewed before the meeting so we would have some idea what we would encounter. We split up the sixteen inmates between the three chaplain interns.

The first woman I interviewed, Ms. Gonzalez, was the leader of the "born agains." She had a "natural life sentence," which meant she had no end date in the computer for her release time, as opposed to other life sentences that actually get translated into years. The problem with having no end date is that a sentence can never be reduced because there is nothing to reduce it from. I was curious as to what this woman had done to deserve such a sentence. I asked one of the chaplains, and he said it had to do with drugs. I said, "Gee, it seems like it must have been more than that." He said, "Well, she was originally from a family in Columbia and there was also a situation of some missing bodies. Let's leave it at that."

Ms. Gonzalez was about five-foot-three with disturbingly deep-green eyes. At that time, we had no Spanish-speaking Protestant minister, and so Ms. Gonzalez had become the de facto prayer leader in a Spanish service from 12:30 pm to 1:30 pm every day. There were a group of inmates who were devotees of Ms. Gonzalez. The women told me that when Ms. Gonzalez first arrived in prison, an angel with dirty blonde hair visited her. Because of the visit she was saved. She was the only one they knew of who had been saved by an actual angel. They all agreed that Ms. Gonzalez had special healing powers. Ms. Gonzalez was also responsible for putting together special newcomer packages for all incoming Latina inmates. The package contained things that could be bought in the commissary, and came with an invitation to join the Christian service and avoid the Catholic service.

As she sat down in front of me, I found her eyes disturbing, and yet for some reason I could not break eye contact with her.

"Ms. Gonzalez, as you know, we are having a problem in the chapel with the Latina community, and I wonder if you would be willing to attend a reconciliation meeting that we are preparing?" I began after a brief silence.

"There is no problem in the chapel," she flatly responded.

"Some of the Catholic women feel that there is." I countered her. "They believe that the Protestant women do not approve of the way that they worship and make it difficult for them to hold their services."

"The Catholic women are too sensitive."

"Well, that may be, but I would very much appreciate your attendance at the meeting." She sat very still and stared at me. She finally responded.

"There is no need for such a meeting because there is no problem. If we hold a meeting it would seem as if we agreed that there is a problem and there is no problem."

I was quiet for a moment, not sure how to proceed.

"In the meeting, we plan to focus on common ground."

"Let me be clear," she said interrupting me, "there is no common ground between us and the Catholics, so there is no problem."

"But don't you think it's strange that it's okay with you that the Wiccans use the chapel and the Muslims use the chapel, and you have no problem with them, but you do have a problem with the Catholics using the chapel for the feast in honor of Our Lady of Guadalupe?"

Ms. Gonzalez glared at me, and her eyes literally changed colors to a deeper green and I could feel the hair on the back of my neck stand up. This was the one and only time I was afraid while I was with an inmate. I sat firmly in my chair, and stared back.

"Since," she said slowly drawing out the word as a blanket to cover her rage, "the Catholics have not been born again; they are not Christians."

"I understand that you believe that," I responded, now feeling more frustrated than afraid. Ms. Gonzalez was very powerful among the chapel inmates, and if she blocked the meeting, I was afraid that people would not attend. I decided to try another tack.

"Why don't you tell me the story of your relationship with God?" I asked, hoping to get us on more neutral ground. She seemed to calm down, and her eyes adjusted once again to a more normal color.

"I was saved while I was in jail, waiting for my trial," she began and spoke easily of her conversion. "It was a very hard time for my family, and I couldn't believe that I had been arrested. The year before my arrest, I was voted 'Mother of the Year' at my children's school, and now this. I was totally broken. I was left in a cell with no one. No family, no friends, no books, no radio, no TV. All I had to read was a Bible left by the Gideons. I read the Bible from beginning to end. I took Jesus into my heart, accepted Jesus as my personal savior, and was saved. I have memorized most of the parts of the Bible, and I know that the Catholic women have not been born again. They were born into Catholicism, which is not their fault, but they must be born again through the blood of Jesus if they are going to be saved. We are talking about their immortal souls, and so this is very important. John 14:6 'Jesus saith unto him, I am the way, the truth, and the life: no man cometh unto the Father, but by me.'" She smiled.

"I see that you have a very solid faith," I began tentatively. "Could I get your agreement that if we have the meeting, you won't interfere? I understand that you will not be able to attend."

"Certainly," she said matter-of-factly. "The women can always do what they want."

After Ms. Gonzalez left, I thought about her and her faith. Was it real or was it contrived to manipulate the women? Maybe it was both. She certainly knew the Bible and spoke of her conversion as reality. It was also a way to control the women. She was the one who led the prayer groups. Her Spanish and English were faultless. I had heard her do simultaneous translation, not an easy thing to do. Each of her behaviors had at least two sides and two impacts. The gift giving could be a sign of true Christian charity and it could be seen as another means of manipulation and bringing people into her fold.

I thought about organizational systems, and how we are all informed and changed by the systems that we enter. We think we can ride above the system, but we cannot. In a prison, women weekly enter and exit the system. The women who have the capability to exert the most influence are those who have been there the longest, and those are the women with the longest sentences. Viewed in these terms, it could be said that the sickest person in the system has the strongest base to influence others. Ms. Gonzalez, with a life sentence, was a fundamental part of the system just as the guards, the staff, and the facility itself were intertwined and could not be separated one from the other.

Several weeks after our interviews, we held the reconciliation meeting. We mixed the Catholic and Protestant groups and asked them to share their faith stories with one another. One of the older Mexican women, who had originally brought the complaint, had the courage to stand up in the group and say she thought it wrong for people to criticize how other people worshipped. She thought people should go to every service where God was invoked. We chaplains affirmed this sentiment. We asked them what they had learned about faith. They offered a variety of responses, including:

"I think my faith is strengthened by seeing the faith of others, no matter what they believe."

"Every morning when I get up I try to remember to say 'Good Morning, God.' Sometimes I don't remember until I am in the shower."

"My faith is strengthened by looking at the mountains, breathing the air, feeling lucky I can get outside. I never see the fence when I am outside walking."

"My faith is strengthened by focusing on others, trying to help them when they are having hard times."

"I have to work on my faith. It is the only thing that will get me through. I will be released in four years. I'll be fifty-seven years old and sent to a country I haven't been to since I was five years old. Only my faith will prepare me."

"The partner I met with has a life sentence. I will never complain to God again about my circumstances. What a spoiled brat I must seem to God."

"I didn't know Catholics believed in miracles too."

In prison, religion is one more thing that inmates can manipulate to gain some sense of power and control in their lives. If I have the power to show that my God is bigger than your God, than I can believe I am bigger than you, and I can also feel like I have some power in a system in which I am powerless. As in the outside world, the underlying tenets of Christianity, to love God and love each other, get lost in the fights of dogma and interpretation. I believe that many of the women I met in prison had a genuine faith that sustained them. I met just as many, however, that used Jesus as their substitution for drugs. They would be "hooked on Jesus." I would question the sustainability of that type of faith once these women return to the outside world.

I learned many things from the inmates. From the radical, I learned, to be reflective about my beliefs. What was I willing to die for? What was I willing to put my life on the line for? This type of metaphysical question had always seemed like a parlor game for me. In prison, I met people whose faith sustained them to a degree that I could not imagine. Instead of being disparaging of their passion, I moved more toward Lori's point of view: that it was remarkable to meet someone who was willing to go to prison for a belief.

In prison, they talk about either doing the time or having the time do you. In much of my life, I felt that the time was doing me. As a child growing up in a scary and chaotic home, I felt each day take its toll on me. I remember how I counted the days until I was eighteen and could be free, just as I saw the women count down the days until their release. As a young woman, I tried to obliterate time by partying, drinking, and plunging myself deep into the river of denial. Many women in prison also tried this approach. Drugs, alcohol, and pills were readily available to them. A few of the women were able to do their time by being in the present moment. They could see and be grateful for all of the little things that made the passing of time easier in prison. They did not dwell on the future. When they woke up in the morning, they tried to remember to say, "Thank you God for this day." I knew I was not in this group, yet, but it was in my consciousness for the very first time. If I could feel liberated by time rather than trapped by it, I believed much of my suffering would disappear.

Chapter Six

MARISA

If you want others to be happy, practice compassion. If you want to be happy, practice compassion. —Dali Lama

I returned from Upaya, and immediately jumped back into my work. The memory of my time at the retreat faded like a dream one has at night and then is absorbed and disappears with the activities of the day. At the time, Silicon Valley was bustling and I was busy doing human resources consulting. Thanks to my contacts at Apple, the work was fairly easy to come by, but without being a part of a company, I found myself again adrift, not sure what I wanted to do, what I was supposed to do, or if any of it mattered.

I began to meditate everyday hoping to regain that sense of bliss I found at Upaya. But, I didn't rediscover it then and haven't since. Instead, I learned that, indeed, my mind was a busy place. I practiced being easier on myself when I lost focus, and I tried to relax. In one of my favorite images, I would imagine myself sitting on a hilltop looking down at a long train chugging by at the bottom of the hill. I had a laughing Buddha on my shoulder. Sometimes, as I sat there, I would find myself riding in an open train car that I labeled train car number three, for planning vacations, or number four for planning dinner parties, or one for wondering what I should be doing with my life. When I realized I was in a car, the Buddha would laugh at me and then I would return my focus to myself on the top of the hill. This approach, for some reason, kept me from being discouraged. I never again meditated for three hours, but I did meditate every day for thirty minutes, and I was surprised at how busy my mind was when no one was watching.

One morning, when I was sitting at the breakfast table drinking coffee, I began reading an article in the morning paper about a woman who started an organization called Jacob's Heart. She started the organization because her good friend's little boy had cancer. She realized the toll that cancer took on the family, and she decided to put together an organization that provided help to other families. I was moved by the story and her courage to jump in and try to help. Her display of kindness to another allowed her to interrupt her life, and reach out to make something happen for the well being of others. Her smiling face in the paper touched me, and I called the number from the article. This woman, Lorene, answered the phone and said she would like to meet me at a restaurant in the Stanford shopping mall.

Lorene was a ball of energy. A former Spanish teacher from the East Bay, she had not only tremendous courage but also a huge heart. I told her that perhaps I could be helpful in raising money for the organization she was starting, but I didn't want to work directly with the kids at the hospital. She told me that raising money was always a great thing to do, and she welcomed my participation. I explained to her that hospitals were a place I avoided at all costs. She smiled and nodded at me. As we finished our salads, she asked me to follow her to her car. Once we got there, she told me to get in and accompany her for a few minutes, while we could continue our talk. She talked about the work and how motivating it was to work with the children and how she had gotten so much more out of the work than she could ever give. I nodded in agreement, and then noticed we were pulling into the driveway at Lucille Packard's Children's Hospital.

"Where are we going, Lorene?"

"I just have a few things to drop off at the hospital."

"Uh, you know, I don't like hospitals. Actually, I haven't been to a hospital since my older sister Diane died, so I really thought that I could just help financially."

"No problem. We really need the financial help, and I appreciate your offer. Could you search in the back seat there and see if you can find a bag of art supplies?" Lorene's car was a large SUV. The back seemed like she had just been to a garage sale and picked up everything she saw. Rummaging through a bunch of bags, I found art supplies, just as we pulled into an empty parking space at the hospital.

"Uh, Lorene, I'll just stay in the car while you go in."

"Don't be silly. We're here now, and I could use your help getting these things out of the car." Somehow her enthusiasm, energy, and force of personality blew right over my feeble resistance. I thought of my experience at Upaya and decided I had the courage to do this. I took a deep breath and followed Lorene in through the glass doors.

We walked into the first floor of the hospital, and I saw a little three-year-old blonde girl pushing a pole that hooked her up to an IV drip. Her parents sat in the lobby, chatting quietly with other parents. I looked into the eyes of the little girl and my stomach lurched. She had such sad, still, and resigned eyes. She was just a baby. I can't do this, I thought. This is too much to ask.

"Susan," I heard Lorene call my name. "Come on, we are going up to the third floor. I want you to meet some people up there."

I took a deep breath and followed her.

The third floor was the oncology floor. We stepped off the elevator and everyone greeted her. Her energy was like sunshine in a dark room. She introduced me to the nurses who worked on the floor, showed me the art room where the kids did art projects and then we started going from room to room as Lorene popped in on every one. She called them by name, dropped off a little present and then went to the next room. I was exhausted just following her. As Lorene stopped to talk to one of the doctors, I saw a young girl who stuck her head around the door to see who was there.

"Hey there," she said. "Come in a minute," and so began one of the major loves of my life.

I hung back for a few minutes, waiting for Lorene, but the young girl waved me in with a big smile.

"I won't bite," she said as I walked into her room.

"What's your name," she asked me.

"Susan. What's yours?"

"Marisa. What are you doing here?"

"I'm with Lorene."

"Lorene's a lot of fun. Do you have kids?""No."

"Do you live nearby?"

"Yes. I live in Palo Alto." This began to feel like an interview.

"Do you know much about kids?"

"Well, a long time ago I used to teach high school English."

Marisa gave me a bright smile that lit up her face. She was a beautiful girl: brown hair, deep brown eyes, perfect white teeth, and olive colored skin. She wore a hospital gown with little, blue, stuffed animals on it.

"Ok," she said, almost laughing. "I guess you're going to do. I don't really have a mom, I mean I do, but she's got problems. I have a grandma, but she gets scared of the doctors. I need someone, and you're the best thing that's come along for me. Will you be my mom?"

"Yes," I said simply.

"That's great. First, you need to know I'm a really social person, so any time you want to come and visit it's good. I'll tell them that you can come any time you want. Is that ok? I can show you around so you'll know where everything is."

"Okay Marisa. I have to go now, but I'll be back tomorrow."

Lorene stood by the doorway, and saw the two of us.

"I guess you'll be coming back to the hospital." Lorene said shaking her head.

"I guess so," I said. Lorene gave me a hug and we continued to deliver presents to other children on the floor.

I lived near the hospital, and so I was able to stop in and visit Marisa three or four times a week. She would ask for things I had never heard of, like chili fries.

"I don't know how to make chili fries, Marisa," I told her after she asked me to bring them to her.

"Mom," she said, and laughed out loud, "No one knows how to make chili fries. You buy them."

"Oh, where do you buy them?" I asked, having no idea where such a thing could be found.

"You know, you get them at the 7-Eleven."

"The 7-Eleven has food you can eat?"

Marisa would look at me and sigh, saying she didn't know how I had gotten through life never having eaten chili fries from 7-Eleven. Of course I got them for her. She made me taste one.

"Disgusting," I said.

"Really? All the more for me." We would both laugh as she ate something I knew was totally bad for her.

"When I get better, I'll cook for you," she told me one day. "I'm a good cook. I make everything with love, and I love you."

"I love you, too, Marisa."

She marked the day we met and kept track of how long we had known each other.

Marisa had acute myeloid leukemia, (AML), a disease of blood cells that results in a rapid growth of abnormal white blood cells in the bone marrow and interferes with normal blood cells.

One day, Lorene stopped me and said she wanted to talk to me about Marisa.

"Susan, I'm not so sure that your working so close with Marisa is such a good idea."

"Why is that?" I asked, feeling instantly defensive.

"You know she has AML, right?" I nodded. "Well, in her case, it is pretty much hopeless. They have thrown everything at her cancer and nothing is slowing it down. I'm just a little concerned about you, and think maybe you might work with some other of the kids that aren't in such a critical condition."

"Lorene, if not her, then who?" I stopped for a minute, took a breath and continued. "I'm in too deep already to turn back." I started to cry for the first time since I had been working with Marisa.

"Okay," Lorene said. "You're an adult. You get to make this choice. Some of the staff is worried that you are getting too close. I'll tell them you understand the risks."

If I hadn't already experienced my sister's death, I might have clung to denial and my hope for a miracle, but I knew in most cases, science trumps faith and miracles. I knew Marisa's chances weren't good, and I knew she was a fighter. If there were a way that someone could beat this disease I believed it would be Marisa. As I tossed and turned, worrying about Marisa in the middle of the night, Joan Halifax's counsel came back to me. We needed to be honest about what was happening, and not be in denial. From that moment on, I believed that being with Marisa now was enough. I didn't need to try to manage our future. Whatever was in store, I felt that I had the faith and courage to cope with it. I would fight my own tendency to escape into the safe land of denial, and try my best to be in the present moment. During the time I was with Marisa, I felt my life was in a universal flow of energy, a feeling I later experienced at the prison.

One day, I walked into Marisa's room and found her grandmother sitting in the room. She lived in Hollister, and it took many bus trips and hours for her to get from her subsidized housing to the hospital in Palo Alto. It was a beautiful summer day, and Marisa was feeling good. She had just had a blood transfusion and wanted to go outside. I went to the front desk and asked if I could take Marisa out.

"You mean outside or out?"

"What do you mean by out?" I asked barely concealing my excitement. "Would you like to take her to the mall? She has been so excited about your visits, and I know she just had a birthday, so maybe a little break would do her good. You know we worry about infections, but if her grandmother will sign her out, you can have her for an hour."

I walked in her room with a big grin on my face.

"Guess what, sweetie pie? We just got permission to escape to the mall for one hour if you want, and your grandmother agrees."

Marisa was beside herself with joy. She hugged her grand-mother who signed her out, and off we went. Marisa had just turned fifteen, and I told her for her birthday I would buy her whatever she wanted.

"I want to go the Gap," she said. "I want to get a hat for my bald head and I want to get a scarf for my throat so that my (stent) marks won't show."

"Okay. Let's go." The three of us walked out of the hospital together and across the street to the Stanford mall.

We walked into the Gap, and I found a young woman to help us. I told her Marisa could have anything she wanted but we only had thirty-five minutes to buy things. I have never seen a happier teenager trying on items, throwing them off, trying on others, and laughing, always laughing.

In the end, Marisa bought one gray knit cap that she used to cover her baldhead, and a white silk scarf. She pulled the cap down over her ears.

"You look like a hoodlum," I told her.

"Great," she said, "better that than some kid with cancer."

"No kidding," I said, while the sales girl seemed uneasy with our patter.

We got back with five minutes to spare. She patted my hand, her most affectionate gesture. Marisa was not one for hugs or kisses. She always worried about infections, and she was very reserved physically.

"Thanks, that was so much fun. I felt like a regular kid."

Unfortunately, Marisa wasn't a regular kid. She would get sent home to Hollister, and then called back to the hospital when her blood count was off. When she came to the hospital, the first thing she did was call me, and I would drive over as soon as I could. Our love for one another deepened with each visit. Marisa was very kind to all of the new kids who showed up on the floor. She explained to them how to fill out their menu cards, and told them they should order food even if you weren't hungry so they would have something to offer to guests who visited. She was fifteen years old, with a terminal diagnosis, and was one of the most gracious people I have ever known.

She told everyone who walked in that I was her mom. One day, she asked me if people could share moms. "I don't think so," I told her. "You are more than a handful of a kid. How could I take on another?" She smiled knowingly at me.

"Hello Marisa's mom," was the greeting I received from each new batch of kids that came in.

When Marisa got treatments and I couldn't go with her, I went to the parent's lounge on the floor. I learned that three other young girls from Hollister had all been diagnosed with AML. How could this be, I asked them, that a disease that is so rare has struck four girls from the same little town? The mothers all blamed the chemicals used on the crops, explaining that they had gotten into the water supply. But no one knew for sure, and there didn't seem any way to prove anything. The women were too exhausted taking care of their children to try to investigate the causes of the disease. When I asked the doctors, they would agree, it was a very rare disease and extremely rare that four girls from the same town were diagnosed, but that was all they could say. You can have all of the theories in the world, but the fact is, they continually told me, we don't know what causes this disease. I eventually stopped asking.

One evening, I stopped in to see Marisa after work. I'd had a really hard day, and I was stressed by my work, and by the traffic I experienced on my way to the hospital. When I walked into Marisa's room, she could immediately feel my stress and took me to task for it.

"Don't be coming in here with your stress," she admonished me. "I don't need that kind of energy around me." I was shocked that she recognized it so quickly and that she called me on it.

"I'm sorry Marisa. You're right. I'll be back tomorrow." I never went into her room again when I was stressed.

When you visit someone with a terminal disease, there is always a fear that when you go to the hospital, no one will be there. Will they call me when she dies, I wondered. But it was too hard of a question to ask, so I would clench my teeth and go up to the third floor searching for her. One afternoon, I walked into her room and she wasn't there. Her bed was made up, but no Marisa. I went to the art room, no Marisa. I walked to the nurse's station and asked where she was. She's having an MRI they told me. She should be back shortly.

When they wheeled Marisa back into her room, I asked her why she went for a MRI.

"They think I'm cuckoo," she said.

"What do you mean cuckoo?" I asked.

"Well, you know how this room used to be Michael's? You know he died in the room last week?" This is a problem with hospitals, people die in rooms and then other people get moved into them.

"No, I didn't know Michael and I didn't know he died. But what has that got to do with you?"

"Well, I saw Michael's ghost at the end of my bed, and it scared me. Then I saw this other old guy. I described him to my grandma and she said it was my grandpa who I've never even met. Like, why would he show up? Anyway, they think I'm coo-coo so they wanted to check my brain and see if I have a tumor." Only at Stanford, I thought.

"Don't worry, Mom. My nighttime nurse told me what to do, so it won't happen again."

"What is that?"

"She told me if I see a ghost again, I'm supposed to say, 'If you don't have a body you're not welcome in my room.'"

"Great idea, Marisa." It was the end of the ghosts, and she did not have a brain tumor.

On another visit, one of the nurses approached me and asked if I could accompany Marisa to the Stanford adult side of the hospital. They wanted to do a test to see if the cancer had spread, and we needed to go to gynecological services. Marisa had been complaining of abdominal pains and they were concerned.

"Marisa is anxious about the exam and we thought it would be good if you could go with her," the pediatric nurse told me. "They have agreed that it will be an external exam only, and I have promised her that she will have a female doctor."

Marisa had to go over in a wheelchair, so I pushed her along and chatted as usual. But Marisa was very silent. I could tell she was in pain and scared.

"It's going to be okay, Marisa," I tried to reassure her. She was always really tough with her pain, but on this day, the pain was beginning to conquer her. Halfway down the halls, as we crossed into the adult side of the hospital, she started to sob. I could feel the pain winning.

"Marisa, look at me," I said and kneeled down in front of her wheelchair. "Look in my eyes and breathe with me." I counted our breaths. Breathe in, one; breathe out, two. I continued with the deep breathing as I had been taught at Upaya, and she started to settle down.

Marisa was very modest about her body. She told me she was still a virgin and didn't want anybody "messing with her privates." I assured her this was not going to happen. Once we arrived in the department, I checked her in and then went back to her.

"Please, take me back. I hurt." I bent over to tell her the procedure would be quick and painless, something the nurses had assured me before we left the children's hospital for our trek over to the adult hospital.

Marisa's eyes challenged me, her face showed the conflict of a fifteen-year-old girl torn between believing her new mom and believing her experience of adults who never told the whole truth.

"Oh, please," she implored, slouching down into her chair, "take me back to the children's side of the hospital. I hate it here. Why do I have to be here?"

"Because, honey, they can't do this type of exam on the children's side." Although I tried to project confidence, I was worried too. I walked up to the reception nurse and asked to see Dr. Macklin. "Is Dr. Macklin a woman?" I asked, bending over, hoping that Marisa couldn't hear me. "No, Dr. Macklin is a man and he is the only doctor on duty."

"But we asked for a woman. Marisa doesn't want this gynecological exam done by a male. We specifically asked for a female." I set my jaw and stared at her, determined to stand my ground.

"I am sorry, but if you want this procedure to be done now, you need to see Dr. Macklin." The nurse left to get the doctor, and I turned to face Marisa.

"Baby, I'm sorry, but they couldn't find a lady doctor. It's a male doctor, but I am sure he is very nice, and it will be okay." I squatted down to have my face next to hers and reached over to dry the tears on her cheeks.

"I hate it here. Why do I have to be here?"

"Because, baby, they need to understand what is causing your pain, and this is the only way for them to figure it out."

A tall, six-foot-three-inch, distinguished-looking man in a neatly pressed white uniform walked toward us. He came over to Marisa, and introduced himself. "I will be giving you your exam, Marisa. Please follow me." I walked along to accompany them.

"I understand that this will be an external exam only, is that correct, Dr. Macklin?"

He stopped walking, and squared off his position, placing himself between Marisa and me. "No, that isn't correct. I explained to the doctors at the children's hospital that an external exam would provide no useful information. We need to do an internal vaginal exam as was first recommended."

Marisa started making a soft mewing sound I had never heard before during all of the tests that she'd had done.

"They promised me," she started cry at the doctor imploring him to be reasonable. Dr. Macklin looked down and said nothing. "You promised me," she said. All her teenage sullenness was now gone, and her eyes held only pain and the defeated demeanor of a fighter who was about to give up.

I checked out the doctor, and my sweet child, and in a moment I made my decision. Even though I had no authority to change hospital procedures, I knew I could do it.

"We're not doing this," I said, and turned Marisa's wheelchair away from the doctor. "We're going back to the children's hospital." The doctor turned to me and shrugged.

"I hate it over here," Marisa cried. "They don't care about people over here. I told you that before." Marisa perked up as we walked back to the children's side of the hospital, commenting on the bright artwork on the walls, her pain, at least temporarily, had disappeared.

At Christmas time, I found some cards that were made to display individual artwork on the front of the card. Marisa had a beautiful sense of color and style, and she would have made a great artist. I brought all of the cards in and sat with her in the art room.

"You have to do yours, Mom," Marisa said as she was going through all of the paints in front of her.

"I hate art work, Marisa. It stresses me out. I have no talent for it."

"Just don't think so much," she told me. "Get the feeling and then paint the card."

Don't think so much, I told myself. How long have I been trying to not think so much?

I started working on a few cards, that were, kindly put, uninspired. Marisa glanced over at my cards and said,

"They're not that bad. Give them to me for a minute." With just two strokes she turned my cards from a stilted mess into something I was proud of. Tears came to my eyes when I saw the change.

"They're just cards," she said, "Wonder what would happen to you if we did a mural?" Again, we laughed so hard we almost got kicked out of the art room.

The doctors sent Marisa home for Christmas, but she had to come back to the hospital in January. When she did, she learned that they couldn't do a bone marrow transplant because they couldn't get her blood count up. As I approached her room, the nurses told me she was in a bad mood.

"Hey, Marisa. What's up?"

"Hi Mom. Nothing. I get nothing but bad news. I hate the doctors that give me the bad news. They never have anything good to tell me. I hate being here. I just want to go home. They told me I have a decision to make; I can go home and get another blood transfusion and go to my Quinceañera, (a special celebration in the Latin American community for girls when they turn fifteen) or I can stay here and go through another round of experimental treatments. What do you think I should do?"

"I don't know, Marisa," I answered, feeling helpless. "What do you think the pros and cons are?" "Well, it would be a good thing to go home and just forget about it. I could go to the dance, go to the mall with my friends, sit with my cat, and see my dad. That would all be good. But, like, what if all I do is stress out that I'm not getting treatment. Then it wouldn't be much fun would it?"

"No honey, it doesn't sound like too much fun."

"It's so unfair that I have to make this decision. I'm too young. Why am I in this mess?"

There was silence between us. Marisa decided eventually to go for experimental treatment in Ohio. They air evacuated her out and back.

When she returned from Ohio, she was rejuvenated. She had never been out of the state of California before, and was fascinated by everything she saw.

"They have those cancer flowers everywhere there," she told when she returned.

"What cancer flowers?" I asked.

"You know those yellow flowers they give out for cancer people. They grow in the ground there and are really pretty."

"Daffodils?"

"Yeah. I don't really like those flowers, but they were pretty there."

One day when I came in, Marisa was in a great mood.

"Guess who I played Uno with today?" she asked me as soon as I sat down on the window seat next to her bed.

"I don't know, but I bet you beat them." She started to laugh.

"I played Uno with Chelsea Clinton. Do you know who she is? She has really curly hair, and she is so nice. Her parents are famous."

"Yes. Her dad is the president. She's going to school here at Stanford."

"Right. Well she had these two big guys with her that stood outside the door. I invited them in but they didn't want to come in the room."

"What did you talk about?"

"Oh, just stuff. She told me she didn't want to be a lawyer like her parents."

"So who won at Uno?" I asked her with a smile.

"She was pretty good. But I beat her on the last game. We had fun. She stayed all the way 'til lunch."

I later asked the nurses about Chelsea, and they told me she didn't want any publicity about her visits; she just wanted to visit the kids. Everyone agreed Chelsea was the nicest of the high-profile people who came into the hospital. Her kindness came through to the children and the staff. In a world of shallow celebrities, Chelsea had managed to keep and nurture her kindness for others.

I was talking to the nurses at the nursing station a few days later when a young woman came out of Marisa's room.

"Who's that," I asked.

"Oh, that's one of our chaplains that comes to visit," they told me.

"You have chaplains that come and visit the kids?"

"Yes, there is a whole department of chaplains that visit here and at the adult hospital."

I asked the woman, Lynn, if she had time to go down for a coffee with me and she said she did.

"So tell me," I asked, "how did you get to be a chaplain?"

"I'm in seminary in Berkeley. It's called Pacific School of Religion (PSR) and is part of a university that is called the Graduate Theological Union. There are nine seminaries in Berkeley. PSR is the nondenominational Protestant seminary. Starr King is the Unitarian Universalist seminary. There is an Episcopal seminary, an American Baptist seminary, a Lutheran Seminary, a Presbyterian seminary, a Jesuit seminary, a Dominican seminary, and a Franciscan seminary. There is also a Buddhist center, and a Jewish studies center. We take classes at all of the different seminaries. It has been the best experience of my life. I loved going to seminary. The locals call the place Holy Hill."

I thanked her for her information and returned to Marisa's room.

"I see you met Lynn," she said.

"Yep."

"Did you like her?"

"I did."

"I call her when it's the middle of the night and I can't sleep. She always comes. She has a soft voice. I like the chaplains. Do you?"

"I do Marisa."

"I know, but do you really like them?"

"Yes, I really like them, but why are you asking me?"

"I don't know; you know I might not be here forever, and I was just thinking about you and what you would do next." This was the first time Marisa acknowledged this to me. "My dad takes pictures of me all of the time, and I know it's so he won't forget me." She gave me a big grin. "I thought maybe you could be a chaplain. That would be really nice."

"Maybe," I said and turned my head away from her. I tried hard to stay present with her, but it was too hard. The thought of her death, her leaving me, was so sad. I didn't want to think about it. My sorrow came up to my throat, and then I changed the subject. But Marisa was done with the topic. She had said what she wanted to say. We never talked about chaplains or chaplaincy again, but the seed had been planted.

Marisa's health continued to deteriorate. The experimental treatment in Ohio hadn't worked, and she was basically being kept alive through blood transfusions.

One day when I arrived, they told me that Marisa had experienced a code blue earlier in the day. Hospitals use this code when a patient needs immediate resuscitation. Marisa later told me about the experience.

"It was so weird, Mom. I could hear them yelling code blue, and then I heard all of this rush around me and then the next thing, I was out of my body looking down at all of them. Then someone pounded me so hard on my chest that I said a bad word, and I was back in my body. Do you think I'm cuckoo?"

"No Marisa, I don't think you're cuckoo, but I wonder if it was scary to be out of your body?"

"Not really. It was just weird."

"I wonder if you are afraid of dying." I finally put the question out there.

"I don't know. I'm getting really tired. It's depressing that I won't be able to do things. Go to dances and meet a boy, shop at the mall. I wish I could grow up and have kids and be like a normal person, but I'm getting tired."

"You know that song "Angel" by Sarah McLachlan?" she asked, "I love that music. It's a little country for me, but the words… Those words are something. Those words are in my head today and won't go away."

Marisa began to sing the song to me accompanied by a keyboard someone had given her.

Spend all your time waiting
For that second chance,
For a break that would make it okay.

There's always some reason
To feel not good enough,
And it's hard, at the end of the day.

I need some distraction,
Oh, beautiful release.
Memories seep from my veins.

Let me be empty,
Oh, and weightless,
And maybe I'll find some peace tonight.

In the arms of the angel,
Fly away from here,
From this dark, cold hotel room,
And the endlessness that you fear.

You are pulled from the wreckage,
Of your silent reverie.
You're in the arms of the angel,
May you find some comfort here.

(Sarah McLachlan. Surfacing. BMG)

Marisa had a beautiful voice colored with the sorrows and emotional suffering she had been through. When she finished, I just sat on her bed staring at her.

"I guess I want that 'beautiful release,' but I don't want to give up, either." She gave me that sly smile of hers.

I sat with her and had such sadness in my heart that I could hardly gather myself.

"You know, Marisa, I did this meditation thing with the Buddhists. I never told you about it but I had my own 'cuckoo' experience."

"Really?" She was one again the fifteen-year-old teenager. "Tell me about your cuckoo experience."

"I did a meditation on death and I felt myself float out of my body. It was really weird, just like you said, but it wasn't scary at all. What I learned is this: death is perfectly safe. There is no more pain, no more suffering, no more waiting. You will be totally safe going over. I promise you this." I said this with every conviction of my being, knowing deep in my heart that it was true.

"Do you believe me?" I asked her. She looked at me for a long time before she answered and finally said,

"Yes, Mom. I do."

Lorene called me a few days later, and told me Marisa had died at home the night before. She was just shy of her sixteenth birthday.

After Marisa died, I felt emotionally depleted. My heart was broken. The other three girls from Hollister who had been diagnosed with AML also died that following year. I tried to provide emotional support to their families; I attended their funerals, and then I decided enough was indeed enough. I felt bereft from the deaths of four teenage girls in two years. I told Lorene that I needed a break from the organization. The organization that she founded, Jacob's Heart, continues to this day to provide services to children who have cancer and their families.

Also, for me, there would never be, nor could there ever be, another girl like Marisa. She was my first daughter, my dear sweet love. She was kind, wise, talented, funny, and thoughtful in spite of her pain. Everyone at the hospital loved her. Her kindness to others engendered a sense of reverence about her. Marisa wrote a letter to my husband Gary thanking him for sharing my time with her. He carries it in his wallet to this day. She and I were a mother and daughter who enjoyed a constant honeymoon. I believed that I was at my best when I was in her presence, and she was always so excited and joyful when I visited her. I was calm, reliable, and focused totally on her. She was, and continues to be, one of the deepest loves of my life. I read somewhere that children's spirits would present themselves as white butterflies. After she died, I sat at my window searching for butterflies as I watched the summer come and go.

Chapter Seven

MY FIVE STONES

People take different roads seeking fulfillment and happiness. Just because they're not on your road doesn't mean they've gotten lost. —Dalai Lama

---

I had a dream that I was sitting in a big empty movie theater waiting for the movie to start. The old-timey theater had swirls of art deco gold and turquoise on the walls, hand-painted, wooden box-beamed ceilings, and a large, raised stage. Crimson velvet curtains trimmed in gold covered the screen and fell in graceful pleats to the bottom of the stage. I sat alone in the theater. Suddenly, the curtains opened and a big God voice boomed in my consciousness, "Susan, I know that you are struggling with the meaning of life, and I want you to know that I have heard your struggle."

In my dream I was delighted. God and I had not had a talk in a long time, and I could hardly wait to hear what he had to say.

"I want you to know that the meaning of life is to simplify it down to these five stones," and with that a huge God hand appeared in front of me holding five various-sized stones. I looked at God's hand, the five stones, and waited. Nothing happened. I was furious. What good is a God who communicates with cryptic answers? I smacked God's hand away from me and told him he was not helpful.

I still felt mad at God when I woke up, and I decided to take the matter up with my therapist. I had been working with her for some time and respected her. She told me she thought it was my responsibility to figure out what the stones represented in my life, and that neither she nor God could tell me the answer. I sat there without saying a word, sure that they both could tell me the answer but wouldn't from some mistaken belief that it was for my own good. Whatever the reason, it was now clear to me that neither God nor my therapist were going to tell me the meaning of life. My therapist told me to find five stones and try to determine the meaning of each one. Although I considered this an inane suggestion, it seemed that my only other alternative was to keep bumbling along on my current path, which had yielded no answers. I decided to be on the alert for any stone that seemed interesting or that I noticed.

I picked up the first stone as I was walking along the banks of the Feather River in Plumas County, California, searching for interesting rocks. I noticed one at the water's edge that seemed to stick out among the others. It was oblong and about two inches long. What caught my eye, were the two thin-lined stripes around the rock. The rock was gray, like slate, but the lines were almost black. I picked it up and it felt smooth in my hand, as if it had been sitting there in the water for eons just waiting for me. I thought, "How like my faith this rock is—oddly shaped, not filled in, but still smooth as silk."

I have come to believe that faith is a gift, like the ability to be psychologically introspective, or the gift for music, math, or languages. I do think it is possible to cultivate our faith. For me my faith deepens when I focus on the positive and nurture a sense of gratitude. How does this build faith? I don't know, I just know that when I am in a space of feeling grateful for my life, I can sense my interconnection to others and the universe. My problems, challenges and limitations seem to shrink in the face of appreciation. For me, my faith is undermined if I let my attention focus on the negative and the black hole of depression. My faith is in something larger than my individual Susan existence, but beyond that I don't have a definition. Whenever I have tried to put it down, it morphs on me and becomes something quite unexpected. I have faith that my life is in a context larger than my own personality, and that my life matters. My faith allows me to relax about my future, but also pushes me to make the most of my life now. I have finally accepted that my definition of faith, like the stone I found will never be filled out.

I found the second stone as I walked in the desert. I was at Upaya the Buddhist retreat center and we were doing a walking meditation. I was trying not to step on snakes or scorpions and trying to be mindful. I was not having much success. My thoughts kept repeating to me how bored I was. For some reason I started to wonder if Jesus were an introvert, since he seemed to like to hang out on boats and in the desert more than with the hordes that followed him. Trying to keep a clear mind, I kept walking, and I saw a pink granite rock, shaped like a leaning baby pyramid. I loved it at first sight. I picked it up and it conformed perfectly to my hand. The bottom was flat, and I could imagine women using it to pound out corn for tortillas or to bop someone on the head. It was strong, and I felt strong when I held it. With this rock, I claimed courage for myself.

I had always been called a scaredy-cat, so it was a new concept for me to think of having courage. Just because I found a rock didn't mean I was actually going to have the courage to stand up for what I believed in, but I realized if I didn't have the courage to stand up for my beliefs either to myself or others, I didn't have any real faith. Faith and courage seemed to go hand and hand and I placed the two stones carefully on my desk.

My third stone was a present to me. One day, when I walked into Marisa's room, she seemed particularly happy to see me. "I have something for you," she said as she held out her hand. "One of the nurses gave it to me, and I knew that it was just for you." It was a small stone, with a white line that resembled a ribbon wrapped around it in a bow. "See, it looks like a gift."

"I see it."

"Well that's what you are to me, a little gift. I want you to have it." I took the small rock in my hand and smiled at her.

How this young woman was able to exhibit such kindness through her pain and medical procedures was astounding to me. Marisa's ability to be kind, to light up the room with her smile, engendered kindness in others. Kindness, the dictionary defines as "a good or benevolent nature." Benevolence is such a big word for such a young girl, but it fits. Marisa taught me the value of kindness regardless of one's own difficult circumstances. Faith, courage, and kindness were the three stones that sat on my desk and it was quite a while before I discovered my fourth stone.

My husband and I had splurged on a vacation to Europe. One of the places we visited was Normandy Beach in France. We hired a guide and took a tour of Omaha Beach and listened as the guide described all of the planning that went into that day, and, yet, despite all of their plans, anything that could go wrong did go wrong. We stood on the beach and gazed across the water, imagining what the sights and sounds were like on that day. I turned around and saw the steep cliffs behind me and understood how impossible the task had been. Yet these young soldiers had no choice but to keep going, knowing they had to cross this beach and in doing so run directly into the face of enemy fire.

We walked up and down the beach, imagining June 6, 1944. I scoured the beach, wanting to find some type of memento to take home. Among many other rocks, on the edge of the shore, I saw a red, triangular-shaped stone that had been churned up in the water. I picked it up and was immediately struck by the color and the texture. This stone, the color of blood that had been exposed to air, had a faint white line, almost like a ghost, in the center of it. I closed my fist around it and the energy emanating from it was so strong that it felt as if it were vibrating in my hands. The ocean had worn it smooth, and it felt like a living thing in my hand. The energy of the stone reminded me of how we all must do what we are called to do no matter how difficult the task. As I held it securely in my hand, I knew that I had just found my fourth stone, and that it stood for service. Mahatma Gandhi said, "The best way to find yourself is to lose yourself in the service of others." Faith, courage, kindness, and service were now rocks that sat on my desk together. It would be several more years before I found the fifth and final stone.

Marisa had not only shown me the path of kindness, but she had also been the catalyst for me to meet other chaplains at the hospital. As I slowly recovered from the sadness of Marisa's death, I thought more and more about becoming a hospital chaplain. I researched the seminary that one of the chaplains told me about. It was across the Bay in Berkeley and was called Pacific School of Religion (PSR). I made the decision that I wanted to go to this seminary, and I applied and was accepted. By the time of the first classes, I felt that I was ready and had healed somewhat after the sadness of losing Marisa. Going to seminary had been something that had been in the back of my mind since I was a little girl. I originally wanted to be a preacher when I was little, but this was not and still is not possible for women in the Southern Baptist faith. To be a hospital chaplain seemed like the perfect next profession for me. I knew it would be difficult since I was 55 years old, and had not been to school for a very long time, but I underestimated the cost in terms of energy and effort.

When I told my friends I was going to seminary, they thought I was crazy. Why did I have to move to Berkeley? Why couldn't I commute from Palo Alto? Why sell my house, leave my friends, my church, everything I had established? The fact was, I was done with that part of my life, and I wanted to move on. One of my friends asked me, "Why don't you sit in on a class at PSR to see what it's actually like?" As it turned out, this was excellent counsel; my response at the time, though, was, "why confuse me with facts?" My mind was made up. I had a spiritual fantasy of a school where people walked around and talked about God, and the meaning of life, and how to find enlightenment. Maybe there is such a place somewhere, out in the golden fields above Big Sur, but that place was not PSR in the year 2000.

After my first week at PSR, I sat on a curb outside the church in tears. I had no idea what I was doing. I didn't know how to select the classes I needed, and if I could identify them, I couldn't figure out how to register. So many things had changed since I had last been in school in the seventies. Computers were omnipresent. Also, everyone at the seminary talked about their call to ministry. If I were called, it must have been in the middle of the night when I was snoozing. I felt like an amateur at a professional tournament. As I sat on the curb feeling sorry for myself, one of my classmates, Kent, came over to console me. He showed me how to choose my classes and how to register. He then led me to the bookstore. He said whenever he was feeling down in the dumps he went to the bookstore. I spent a lot of time there.

The seminary admissions office warned me the course work would be academically challenging, but I blew them off. I had an undergraduate degree in English, a master's degree in psychology. How hard could a master's in divinity be? I had no idea. First, I had to learn an entirely new vocabulary: social justice, exegesis, hermeneutics, and epistemology. I spent more time with my dictionary than I did with the material I was supposed to be reading. Next, the kids in my class were babies who had just come out of undergraduate degrees in biblical studies. They were smart, opinionated, and well spoken. Sitting with them at lunch, I didn't understand their jokes, their slang, their music, or their worldview. On top of that, I didn't know the Bible as well as I thought I did, as evidenced by my shock that David and Solomon were related.

At least I knew I was a decent writer. As an English major, I had received positive comments on my writing and critical thinking. My first assignment at PSR was to write two pages interpreting one Bible verse, using textual criticism as the method. I waxed on, in what I thought was a creative interpretation. I received a "0" on the paper for not following guidelines and missing the point of the exercise—the first of many shocks.

In my first theology class, one of my fellow seminarians surprised me when he declared that he didn't believe in God, but was there to do social justice work through the black church. What?

This very smart young man later became one of my best friends. One day, he said to me, "One of the things we learned from your generation was that to do work in the African American community it is important to work through the churches. Your people didn't do that, and that was one of the problems with the sixties."

My people? Right. I didn't tell him that I spent the sixties partying in Tennessee and then trying to escape a revolution in Libya when that nutcase Gaddafi took over.

I survived my first semester by studying all the time. I learned that because I was 55 years old I couldn't procrastinate and pull all-nighters. My work had to be complete by dinner, or my brain would be the consistency of runny oatmeal, where nothing would stick. I had signed up for 12 hours of classes, another mistake. I found out that most other students had only signed up for nine hours the first semester. Other than time I spent in class, I was at the library or deeply immersed in a religious world previously unknown to me. I finished my first semester with top grades, and realized the young ones and I were now on an even playing field. My life experience began to balance against their fervor and intellectual quickness. I learned to respect the Bible in ways that I had never known. We were taught to read the texts in the context of the period in which it was written. Many people, particularly fundamentalists, had their faith shaken in the first year. For me, the opposite was true. I developed a deep and abiding understanding of the many ways that faith operates and sustains us in our lives.

The second year, we were required to take a course in field education. For most students, this meant they would have their first experience as ministers. Most of the students took positions as youth pastors. I came to seminary to become a chaplain. I had no interest in or illusions about being a leader in a church community. There was a Children's Hospital in Oakland that had an opening for an intern, and I was sure that I was supposed to be there. I called daily to ask about applying for their internship program. No response. I emailed. No response. Talk about knocking on the door! Eventually, everyone in my class had an assignment but me. My professor gently said, maybe the hospital isn't the right assignment for you. I explained to her about Marisa and how I felt I was now able and wanted to help other kids. She told me to try again. I called, left messages, and, again, received no response. Finally, I gave up. By this time only one assignment remained posted on the wall—an internship at a federal prison for women. I shuddered at the thought. I talked to my best friend Linda who said, "You're, already over there, why not go for it? You've made the leap; you might as well immerse yourself in it. It's only for a semester. Five months. How bad could it be?"I took down the 3x5 card from the bulletin board and called the number. Chaplain Becker answered on the first ring.

Chapter Eight

SEX IN PRISON

The best sex I ever had was during my time in prison. —Heidi Fleiss

When I told people I was going to work in a federal prison for women, a look of horror and fear would cross their face. When asked about women in prison, most people think of a black and white Grade B movie, where women hold onto the bars of their cells and wail into the face of the audience. There is something about this image that is both lurid and titillating, even if it has no basis in reality, so the image remains.

The federal prison where I worked was nothing like this, and yet the oppressiveness of the system engendered a feeling of repression, fear, and control. People have referred to the effect of being in a woman's prison as experiencing "pastel fascism." As the chaplains would say the punishment for the women is in being away from their families and loved ones. The prison itself does not need to create any further punishment. Not everyone within the prison hierarchy shared this philosophy.

Women's prisons are different from men's prisons in substantive ways. Generally men who are in federal prisons are incarcerated for having been convicted of committing violent crimes. Prison rules are established to protect the men from the predatory practices of one another including sexual aggression. The men form subcultures to provide a barrier between them and the guards and one another. Since women who are in a federal prison are mainly incarcerated for drug offenses, there are a very small percentage of them who are considered violent. Female subcultures are formed, like the men, to provide a barrier against the staff, but not as protection against one another. As a matter of fact, subcultures are created to provide an emotional support system for one another. This need for emotional connection is essential in understanding the social climate of women who are incarcerated.

Because there are only four federal prisons for women in the United States, many women are incarcerated more than a day's drive from their families. This means that many women do not receive visits from their families, or probably anyone else. Additionally, men who are in prison generally receive regular visits from the women in their lives, but when the women are the one's inside, men do not visit with the same frequency as women will visit men. There are some husbands and boyfriends that show up for the women, but this is not the usual experience.

The majority of women in prison have children and until their incarceration, they were the primary caregivers. The women try to stay connected to their families through frequent calls home, mail, and in person visits when possible. Since the women do not have access to computers because of security concerns, email is not an option for them. Many of the women maintain very strong relationships with their children but other women maintain no relationship at all. The grandparents often become the caregivers for the children. The grandparents generally try to keep the children involved with the lives of their mothers, but it is a complicated undertaking. Some of the children are ashamed that their mothers are in prison, other children remain angry with their mothers for the behavior that landed them in prison. The women learn that trying to maintain discipline of your child from inside a prison is impossible. The power in the relationship is with the children and their caretakers not the mothers. Mother's Day and Christmas were the saddest days at the prison. On Christmas Day the chaplains presided over multiple services, but it was difficult to get the women to attend. Most of them coped by pretending these holidays were just another day on the calendar.

I saw a posting on the bulletin board for a meeting on "Coping with Life." I initially thought this was for the women to learn "life coping skills." I quickly learned that this was a support group for women with a life sentence. For women who had a life sentence, developing a coping strategy was vital for their survival. Some of the women with life sentences coped by retreating into an imaginary world; others coped by becoming the "Queen Pins" of the compound. They said the hardest part for them was to see people leave the institution every Friday, knowing that it would never be them. It is also important to keep in mind that the crimes these women committed in order to get a life sentence were horrific, and their punishment also, to me, was horrific.

Although the women were warned in orientation to avoid being "gay for the stay," many of them ignored this piece of counsel. Most women have a need to be in relationship, and with male visitors scarce and relationship with the male guards strictly forbidden, many women turned to one another for a loving relationship. Many of the women became couples and encountered typical couples' problems with communication, independence and dependence, and jealousy. Although the relationships may have started out being sexual, most of them settled into relationships that were based more on companionship than sex, although the temptation of illicit sex was always there. Not all women chose to be "gay for the stay." Some of them were strongly committed heterosexuals and firmly rebuffed any attempts to get them into gay relationships. I never heard of a woman who was coerced into having sex with another inmate.

During my time as a chaplain, I was asked to do couples counseling with some of the women that I saw, and I agreed to see both of them in my office. The things that were brought into these sessions were similar to relationship issues on the outside; not spending enough quality time with one another, being too dependent or too independent, not stating one's needs clearly and in a way that is actionable. There were many couples that stayed together for their entire time of incarceration and just as many who broke up during their time together. They would speak of their relationship continuing on the outside, but it always sounded more like a fantasy, as if both women knew that this relationship existed only within the confines of the institution.

Women also created entire prison "families." The most common relationship was mother/daughter. If a young woman came into the institution, she was often assigned, "parental units" by the other inmates to help take care of her, to make sure that she stayed out of trouble, but most importantly to give unconditional emotional support. If the woman was having a bad day, or received tragic news from home, or was having problems with one of the prison staff members, the prison "mothers" were there to help. It gave meaning to some of the women with longer sentences and it helped the younger women through the transition of living an institutionalized life.

This is not to say that all was rosy with the prison family situations. There would be prison "divorces" with the designated children not knowing which parental unit to side with or how to accommodate both sides. Additionally there was the matter of sex in the rooms. Although sex was outlawed by the prison regulations, it went on everywhere in the institution but primarily in the rooms. With three or four women to a room, there was always conflict about privacy. I had many women tell me that they hated being in their rooms because their room mates were having sex and there was nowhere else to go. No one told the guards unless they were willing to suffer the consequences of being outcast.

If the women were caught having sex by a guard they were sent to the SHU (Special Housing Unit) or solitary confinement. Women who spent time there were confined to their cells (these were truly cells) for 23 out of 24 hours every day. They were let out for one hour a day for exercise in what resembled a dog run.

There was no natural light in the rooms and no ability to program any events. I once went to visit someone who was in the SHU for some infraction. They pulled her out of her cell in handcuffs and her legs were chained. She was so embarrassed to have me see her that way that she only put her head down and would not talk to me. After that incident, I only visited on a walk through basis, asking the women if they wanted Bibles, or other religious reading material. This was the only reading material they were allowed.

I never heard of a woman being raped by another woman. I never heard of a guard raping an inmate, although I am sure this occurred. I did hear numerous tales of inmates who were having affairs with the guards, but it was always presented as mutual. I cautioned the women against these types of relationships as each one I knew of came to a bad end. Generally the other inmates would be jealous of the inmate and the guard, and would turn in the inmate that was having the affair. This would result in the woman either being sent to the SHU or being sent to another institution and the guard being reprimanded or fired.

Still sex in prison was and I'm sure continues to be a coping mechanism. Not all women who pared up had sexual relationships Women's need for relationship and affection is not extinguished because they are put in prison. I have been told by many male staff that female inmates are much more difficult to manage than male inmates. The women are less obedient, more defiant, more emotionally needy, and more manipulative than the men. I believe it.

Chapter Nine

CONFESSIONS AND REMORSE

The U.S Court of Appeals for the Fifth Circuit has held that "lack of remorse" and "acceptance of responsibility" can be separate factors and that a district court may consider each independently of the other.—U.S. vs. Douglas

The psychology intern came in, threw her file folder on the desk, and plopped down in a chair opposite me.

"Had a bad session?" I asked her. This was her first semester at the institution. She was young, passionate, and naïve.

"I guess you could call it that," she said, clearly disgusted. "I just found out that the intake I completed on one of the inmates was totally made up. I spent three hours with this woman, taking down all of my notes, and then I found out that every single thing she told me was a lie. Why would someone do such a stupid thing when I can check out all of the facts in her file? Why would she lie to me like that? What a waste of my time. How do you deal with this?" she asked, clearly exasperated.

I sat back to think for a few minutes. How did I deal with it?

"Well, my situation is a little different. First, I never know the facts of the people I work with, so I never actually find out that I have been lied to. Second, I'm not a psychologist; I'm a pastoral counselor. I think if they are lying to me they are lying to God and God has more knowledge about all of this than I do."

"I don't know, Susan. Sometimes I think we are both just wasting our time here."

It was something I also wrestled with. How much good was I doing? My first goal was like a doctor, to do no harm. Next, I wanted the women to see someone who cared about them and their circumstances. I referred to it as showing them the female face of God. Was that enough? Did my presence with them make any difference, or was I just an excuse for them to get out of their work assignments or break up the monotony of their routine? At this point the answer was unclear.

The following week, I was in a group with my friend Lori and the other chaplains. Lori had a situation she wanted to talk about. She had a woman who came in and said that everyone in her life had given up on her. Her mother had given up on her, her sister had given up on her, and her children had given up on her. The inmate's question to Lori was, "When will the Lord give up on me?"

I jumped into the discussion and said that God would never give up on her. I said I was sure God loved her and forgave her.

Chaplain Becker slowly turned to me and said, "How do you know that Chaplain Pohl?" I was once again in CPE training.

"Well, God forgives everyone. That's what I believe."

"So God forgives everyone whether they have asked for forgiveness or not?"

Now I had that "I'm on thin ice" feeling. Trying to debate these theological concepts with Lutherans is always more than a little bit tricky.

Luckily for me Lori responded.

"I didn't ask her if she had asked for forgiveness. I wanted to reassure her. I told her God would never give up on her."

"What prompted you to tell her that?" Chaplain Becker asked. "Because I didn't want her to think that God would abandon her. I wanted her to have some hope."

"Where does repentance fit into that?"

As soon as Chaplain Becker said that word, I could feel my skin crawl. All those backwoods preachers in Tennessee would use repentance as a whip to get people into shape. As I later learned as a child, "Prepare to meet thy Maker" means you should repent immediately or you were going to burn in hell forever. I felt irritated with Chaplain Becker and myself. Repentance had always terrified me. If I bought into the repentance idea, it seemed to me, I also bought into the idea of hell, and the idea of hell from a child raised a Southern Baptist was the scariest idea of them all. I tried to change the theological tenor.

"Unity says that sin is "Self-Inflicted Nonsense." I said, hoping to divert the conversation.

"Well then, how do you explain evil?" Chaplain Becker instantly countered. "You think the things these women have done are nonsense? You think the beating of that baby was nonsense?"

Clearly not. I realized once again that I was stumped. Where did repentance fit into a world of a loving God? Was I the person who was supposed to tell the women they needed to repent? Did God's forgiveness come whether or not they repented? What were the psychological ramifications of repentance? What was my real purpose here as a chaplain? Was it to make the women feel better by reassuring them that someone cared about them? Was it to provide some solace in a brutal system? What was the service I had committed to and did it make any difference in the larger scheme of things? Was the psychology intern right in that we were all wasting our time with these women?

"So," I started to talk once again as a way to sort out my thinking, "are you telling me that our purpose as chaplains is to get the women to repent? I don't think that's part of my charter. I don't think I believe in the necessity of repentance in order for God to love us," I answered, not sure any more what I believed.

"It depends upon how you define repentance," Chaplain Becker responded. "For me, it's important for these women to tell the truth about what they did wrong. That would be the confession part. And then to say they would never do this again; that's the repentance part. Then ask for forgiveness. Can you see that you can't just tell them they are forgiven if all they do is say I did this crime, and you say ok, God forgives you?"

I sighed deeply. This was a Lutheran answer, but I felt reluctant to use it as my answer. I didn't want to put the women on a "hot seat" where they were made to confess. It felt somewhat like the Christianity of the Inquisition to me. I could see that what I was proposing could be interpreted as "cheap grace," as a Lutheran theologian called it. Did I believe that forgiveness was possible without repentance or confession? If God is love, than forgiveness should flow regardless of our defenses, right?

What was my part in this? Was it good enough to show the women that I cared about them? Was I here to reinforce the status quo of their lives, but support them in such a way that they felt a little better about themselves? As a person of faith, did I have a responsibility that was different from that of the psychology intern? All of my rebellion against my Southern Baptist upbringing was clouding my theological perspective. Chaplain Becker said the first step was to have them tell the truth, or to hear their confession. Did I believe in the doctrine of confession? No. Did I think it was beneficial to hear their life story without judgment and with a compassionate heart? Yes. What was the difference between the two, semantics, or something deeper?

If I agreed with the first step of Chaplain Becker's theology, how could I create an environment, with women who lie about everything, in which it was possible to tell the truth? The psychology intern had no luck in getting her client to tell the truth. At a deep level I understood this. In my family, telling the truth resulted in punishment. Maybe it was the same here. What would it have taken in my family for us to tell the truth about what we had done wrong? I think I would have told the truth if there were no punishment, but I never trusted that if I did something wrong, and then told the truth about it, it would be to my benefit. Truth and fear were not very easy companions.

I decided that establishing a trusted connection and a bond was the first step in creating an environment where truth had a chance to be heard. How did I go about developing a relationship in this environment? Could the women ever learn to trust me? Could I ever learn to trust them? What was trust? At least I had a sense of the answer to this question. Trust to me was in part a reliance on the integrity of what they were telling me. Was that possible in this environment? If I blindly believed everything they said, and put the truth in God's hands, as I had said to the psychology intern, how would I develop and receive trust? Did I just trust that trust would develop?

I returned to my office after this discussion to find a young Native American woman waiting for me. She had long, straight, black hair, a round face, and a timid manner.

"Hello Chaplain Pohl, my name is Amber. Do you have time for me?" she started in a very soft voice.

"Yes, certainly I do. Please come in. How can I help you?"

"I don't know really. I don't know if anybody can help me. I did a really bad thing and now I'm here. I'm nineteen years old, and I feel like my life is over. I'm also seeing people in psychology, and they suggested I come and talk with you, so here I am."

Her eyes held such deep pain and sorrow that it was hard to believe she was only nineteen years old.

"What would you like to talk about?" I asked.

"I think I want to talk about my grandmother. I have been dreaming about her a lot lately. She had a big house where all the kids would gather. My grandmother didn't drink and so her house was always safe. She wouldn't let any adults in her house if they'd been drinking, but little kids could go in any time. She taught me to cook, and sew, and bead. I have been working on my beading again since I have been here. Want to see what I've done?"

I nodded.

She took out an exquisite; half-finished; red, white, and black necklace. The beads were tiny and perfectly lined up. Her artwork was exquisite.

"That's lovely," I said.

"Thanks. I'm doing it for my mom. Not my real mom of course, my prison mom. I call her and her friend my parental units." We both smiled at this reference.

"So do your parental units watch over you here in prison?"

She laughed, and her whole face brightened.

"Yes. They try to watch out for me because I'm so young. I think I'm about the youngest person here. Inside we get a new family. I now have my parental units, aunts, uncles, cousins, brothers, and sisters. I needed a new family, and now I have one." She smiled briefly, and then the sadness returned to her eyes.

"Psychology said I was depressed, but my parental units said who wouldn't be depressed to be in prison. What do you think? Do you think everyone here is depressed?"

"I don't know Amber. Are your parental units depressed?"

"No. I don't think they are, but they're very old. They must be at least 50."

I smiled at that thought.

"I guess I should tell you why I'm depressed, the reason why I'm in here."

"If you want to," I responded"There was an accident. I was driving. I had five kids in the car with me: my two sisters, my brother, and two of their friends. We stopped at the 7-Eleven store on the reservation for me to buy beer for everyone, since I was the oldest. We sat in the parking lot and drank a few beers and listened to music. Then, we decided to drive across the reservation to a friend's house. Something happened, I still don't know what, but I lost attention for just a minute, and the next thing I knew there was a semi-truck right in front of me. I tried to turn the wheel to the left to miss it, but it struck the car broadside. I don't remember anything except flashes of metal and terrible sounds. When it was over, I got out of the car. I didn't have a scratch on me. There were bodies everywhere. I started to try to find my little sister, but I couldn't find her. I think I blacked out. An ambulance took everyone away, including me. When I woke up in the hospital, it was all over. I asked the nurses about the other kids. They told me they were all dead. My baby sister who trusted me, my friends—everyone was gone. It was the way the car turned. I turned the car away from the truck to the left, and it hit the passenger side of the car. It didn't hit my side. It hit the passenger side and then rammed the back. It happened so fast. After the accident, my parents wouldn't talk to me. They said I was the oldest and should have known better, and that I killed half my family."

I sat in silence, considering the enormity of her suffering and the suffering that she had caused.

"The tribe shunned me."

"What does that mean?"

"It means they wouldn't have anything to do with me. All during the trial, no one spoke to me, and I didn't speak to anyone. There were arguments about my situation because of my age. I was eighteen, but had just turned eighteen the week before. The trial took a year. The lawyers tried to get me sent to rehab because I was so young, but they sent me here. I only had two beers, but I drank them fast, and so I tested high on that test they give you. They said I killed five people, and I did. I never tried to defend myself; there was no defense.

"During all of that time, only two people spoke to me, my grandmother and Shawn, a boy I dated. Shawn came to the trial every day, and he sends me mail here. We saw each other every day while I was waiting to come in. We would sit at his house, drink beer, and listen to music. He told me writing isn't so easy for him, but he tries. He writes me little notes trying to cheer me up. I got a very light sentence, only fourteen months. I have nine months to go.

"When I am alone, I hear the sounds of the accident, the metal; I see the flashing lights and the bodies. I dream about it at night. Last night, I dreamed I was with Shawn, but I didn't want to be. I told him to go away. I am walking down a long road, and I see my sisters and brothers who were killed. I am happy to see them alive. I put my little sister down in the water, and then I let go of her, like I'm drowning her. I sit on the road and I'm crying. Next, I'm in a boat in my nightgown and I'm crying. People on the shore are chanting, "we saw you do it." I ask them to bring my brothers and sisters back, but they keep chanting "we saw you do it." I wake up.

"I wish I could have hugged them, even in a dream, but the dream always ends badly. Psychology said I needed to deal with my grief and that maybe you could help, but I don't know what you can do." She hung her head as she turned away from me.

"Sometimes it helps people to talk through their grief. Sometimes it is hard for other people to listen to another person's sadness and regret, but I can do that for you. Why don't we meet every week for a while, and we can see where it goes," I said to her. "It's important for you keep your appointments with psychology and I will put you on the call-out sheet (a form used to give inmates permission to attend different meetings) to meet with me. Ok?"

"Yeah, sure. It's ok."

When Amber left, I knew that I would need to talk to the head of the psychology department. In the outside world, two people counseling one person would be considered an ethics violation. I was uncertain how this situation would be handled inside the institution. A natural tension existed between the Psychology Department and the Religious Services Department. Although the people in the departments respected one another, there was an underlying suspicion about the beliefs and values that each held. Being a chaplain intern, and interested in counseling, I tried to cross the boundaries between the two departments. When I discussed Amber with the head of the psychology department, he said that since I would not have access to the inmate's files, and

Amber agreed to see me and the psychologist, he did not see it as a conflict. We agreed that I would focus on her grief, and the psychology department would focus on her drinking and her guilt. I agreed to the parameters, although I thought that her guilt was also part of the pastoral work. He agreed that things were never as cut and dried as they seemed, and we would check in with each other after a couple of months.

Several weeks later, I was pleased to see Amber on my call-out sheet. I hadn't seen her for a while, but I had heard good news from psychology that she was doing well in her addiction class. She had just celebrated her twenty-first birthday. When Amber came in, she seemed like a very different young woman than the depressed girl who had told me about the accident that had killed her sister and friends. She appeared upbeat and happy. She had just gotten a letter from Shawn, her boyfriend, who was planning to see her when she was released in six months.

"Hi, Chaplain Pohl. It's good to see you. I've been really busy taking classes, and I just got the best news."

"What's that?" I asked. "I can always hear good news."

"I got my test scores back, and I just passed all of the sections of the GED!"

"Congratulations, Amber."

"Yeah it's really cool, because I'm now the only one in my family who is a high school graduate. I feel so proud of myself. I'd like to come back next week if that's ok. I'm starting to really think about what I want to do when I get out."

"Sure, put your name on the call-out sheet."

A few weeks later, Amber showed up again, and said she was fighting with her parental units.

"What are you fighting about?" I wondered.

"They're mad at Shawn because I gave my money from the tribe to him, and he wrote and said he was sorry, but he drank all the money away. They think I should have the money sent to my family, but they would just drink it away, too. I can't have the tribe money sent here, so what's the difference? Shawn needs it. We love each other. The only thing that keeps me going here is knowing that he is waiting for me."

"What do your parental units say about this?"

"They say I should break up with him because if I see him on the outside, I'll start using again. I promised them that I wouldn't. I can just have a few beers and not get in trouble. It isn't Shawn that's the problem; it's me. They say he'll make it harder for me."

Later that week, I received a call at home from the chaplain's office asking if I could come in a day earlier. There was a problem with Amber, and they wondered if I could come in to see her. As I got dressed—same old navy blue pants, looped belt to secure the chain that held my keys, badge pinned carefully to my striped blouse—I thought about Amber. She had seemed to be on the right track. She had graduated, and was planning for her upcoming release. What could have happened that was so urgent that they called me? The office had never done this before.

When I got there, I went directly to Chaplain Becker's office.

"What's going on with Amber," I asked, barely disguising my rising fear.

"Is she one of the people that you see?"

"Yes. I've seen her intermittently. She's also seeing people in the psychology department."

"She's on suicide watch," he said, as he rifled through his papers.

"What happened to her?" I asked.

"It seems there was an accident on the reservation and the boy she was dating…

"Shawn?"

"Yes," he said, "that was his name. He was riding in the back of a pickup truck on a dirt road in the back of the reservation, and the truck sped around one of the curves, and he flew out the back of the truck, struck his head on a rock and was killed. They told her yesterday, and she has been on suicide watch ever since. Have you ever talked with anyone on suicide watch before? No. Well, it's basically a backroom at the clinic where they can monitor her on TV 24/7. There are inmates who are trained by psychology to sit with other inmates on suicide watch. One of the native women is with her. She asked to talk to you, which is why I thought it might be a good idea for you to come in a day early. It's probably a good experience for you. You up for it? " He asked, checking me out slowly as I nodded yes.

I headed over to the clinic and was processed in by the officer on duty. I walked into the room and saw Amber sitting in a chair with her head down. She reminded me of a horse, that you see in cartoons sometimes that has been hit in the head and is dazed and nodding its head up and down. Her long hair covered her face, and she sat slowly rocking herself.

I knelt down in front of her.

"Hi Amber, it's Chaplain Pohl." I leaned toward her, trying to establish eye contact.

The room seemed cold to me. The white linoleum, the cameras in the corner, and the windows that opened into another office reminded me of an interrogation room you would see on TV.

"Amber," I tried again to get her attention through her medicated haze. "Can you hear me?"

Amber finally acknowledged me and smiled.

"I can hear you, Chaplain Pohl," for some reason this reassured me immensely.

"Amber, they said you wanted to talk to me." She seemed to try to focus her eyes on me. She sighed, took a deep breath, and began.

"Chaplain, do you think that God punished me by killing Shawn? Do you think he died because of me?"

This question is the ultimate question brought about by retribution theology, the idea that God takes retribution upon us for the sins we have committed. This was a theology that was prevalent in the Old Testament, but was not part of Christian theology in the

New Testament. When Jesus met a man who was born blind, his disciples asked him who had sinned, the man or his parents? Jesus replied neither had sinned. In my experience, most of our punishment is truly self-inflicted.

"Amber, listen to me? Think about God. We say God is..."

"Love," she answered.

"Do you believe that God loved Shawn?"

"Yes," she answered slowly. "I believe God loves all his people."

"Think about this Amber, if you were all-loving, would you kill someone to punish someone else?"

"No, I would never do that."

"Then how could you think God would?"

"I don't know, but then why did it happen?"

"I don't know Amber. I just don't know." I could feel tears well up in my eyes, as her pain began to break through the drugs.

"I am so sorry, Amber. I am so very sorry." Amber put her hand over her mouth and started to rock again.

"You don't think this was my fault?" she asked me once again.

"I absolutely do not think this was your fault. You are doing the best you can inside here, and you need to continue on that path. Is that right?"

"Yes, Chaplain Pohl."

"Are you going to be all right? Am I going to see you tomorrow at our regular time?"

"I'm going to be all right. I'll see you tomorrow."

I headed out to my car, incapable of stopping to talk to Chaplain Becker. How could so many horrible things happen to one girl? Where was God in this? Was God just sitting on the sidelines like I used to believe? Why didn't I have better answers? If there were no answers, why did we all so desperately want them? Was everything just random? The faith that had sustained me started to waiver. If we are all just victims of our fate and social context, where can and does religion fit into it? Is it as Karl Marx said, "the opiate of the masses"? Is that what I was doing? Dispensing opiates?

When I got home, Chaplain Becker called to check on me.

"I thought I would check to see how you are doing," he explained.

"I'm ok, a little depressed about Amber's situation."

"Let's talk about this tomorrow. I just thought you should know that they took her off suicide watch. She is still medicated, but they moved her back to her room."

"Thanks for calling me, Chaplain Becker."

My questions remained. How much choice do we actually have, depending on where or to whom we are born? It seemed that just when Amber was beginning to escape the clutches of her fate, something would happen to drag her back again into the maelstrom of grief, sorrow, and addiction.

When I returned to my office the following day, a new inmate had come in to see me. Her name was Helen, and she was also Native American. She worshiped with a Shaman from her tribe, but she said she had a very specific purpose she wanted to work on with me. Helen was about fifty years old, tall and elegant, and moved with a sense of grace and purpose. Her long, dark hair was graying at the front, and she had gathered it into a neat bun at the back of her neck. She had been in the prison for over thirty years. She was serving a life sentence, but she had entered the institution when parole was still possible under the federal guidelines; however, every time she came up for parole, it was denied, because of the seriousness of the "incident."

The more she talked about the incident, the more reluctant I felt about hearing her description of something that had happened over thirty years ago. With a life sentence, I knew that her crime had to have been significant. Even though I had heard Amber's story, this felt different. At the end of our first session, I still didn't know anything about the incident.

At my next meeting with Chaplain Becker, I told him about my resistance to hearing her story.

"I wonder what you are afraid of, Chaplain Pohl?" he asked.

"I don't know; maybe I'm not strong enough to hear her story. Maybe the story will stay with me in some unhealthy way. Maybe I will see her as a criminal instead of someone I can help. I wish I could just avoid this. Do you think I should just wait and see if she volunteers to tell me about the incident? I don't think I need to ask her about it, do you?"

"First of all, I want you to know that I do understand how hard this is. It is difficult to hear stories of crimes, and you are new at the institution. Second of all, just because you ask her to tell you, doesn't mean that she will. Yet, for whatever reason, you are here with this woman now. I think it is important in your role as chaplain to hear her story, if she wants to tell it." I told him I agreed, and would try to have courage and ask her about the incident the next time I saw her.

The next week when I returned to the institution, Helen came in again to see me, and again was talking about her parole and the problems with the incident. Midway through the session, I asked her if she wanted to tell me about the incident, and she said yes.

She told her story in great detail; as if she were describing a movie she had recently seen. Although I have changed a few details, this is basically the story she told me.

She told her story in great detail; as if she were describing a movie she had recently seen. Although I have changed a few details, this is basically the story she told me. She told me that the weather on the reservation had been particularly hot and dry that month and that she and her friends were bored. There was no work for the men and no work for her. She had two children under the age of five, and they were demanding and often sick. On that day, she decided to leave her children with her mother, even though she knew her father would start drinking and sometimes beat her mother. She worried about the kids being with them, but she just wanted to get away. She wanted to get out with other young people and have some fun. There was a group of four friends, two men and two women. No one had a car or any means of transportation, so they decided to walk into town and into a bar early in the morning. They walked the three miles in the cool morning sun. They had fun as they walked along together, telling stories, being silly, imagining if they came into a lot of money what they would do with it.

At around 10:00 in the morning, they had their first round of beers. The bar was cool and dark and there were a lot of other native people. They played darts, and cards, and kept drinking. They ran out of money around 4:00 pm, and decided to walk back home in the heat of the day. One of the men said he knew a short-cut across the canyons. They were so drunk, they could hardly stand, but they followed the man who said he knew the way. She said everyone started complaining about the heat, and how they wished they had stayed at the bar. The man who led them was getting angry and said they would be home soon, but the farther they walked the longer it seemed. Finally, they saw a truck in the distance coming toward them. The man said, let's hijack the truck and drive ourselves home. They all agreed to it. They decided the women should stand in the middle of the road and wave the truck down and ask for help, and the men would hide in a ditch beside the road.

The women stood in the middle of the hot, black asphalt road, and flagged down the truck. When the truck stopped to help the women, the men jumped out of the ditch, went to the driver's side, and screamed at the driver to come out of the truck, but the driver wouldn't open the door. The two women stood in front of the truck so that the driver would have to run over them in order to move. The men finally broke open the driver's door. The driver still wouldn't get out of the truck. One of the men reached in to grab the driver and another man held the driver down. Then, in a flash, the first man took a knife and slit the driver's throat. There was blood everywhere. Helen said she started to sober up when she saw the blood and realized they had just killed a white woman.

They all started yelling at each other. Finally, one of the men put the woman in the truck and then drove it over the side of the canyon. He walked back up the long hill from the canyon as they all stood and watched him. He made them each take an oath of silence about what had happened. They walked back to their homes, still drunk from the beer, the heat, and the violence. The next night, they were all picked up and arrested. Helen and the other woman never broke their oath of silence. They were given life sentences. The man who killed the woman, and the other man, both turned state's evidence and were given reduced sentences. The men are both out of prison.

Hearing her story left me feeling exhausted, and slightly nauseated. The pain and suffering of so many people was hard to listen to, even if it had occurred thirty years before. My heart felt broken, and, as I feared, the story has never left me. Trying to reconcile the violence of the crime with the quiet, graceful woman who sat across from me, created a deep cognitive dissonance within me. This dissonance remained with me for the entire time I worked with the women in prison. How could these women, who I had come to know and love, have done these cruel acts?

Several weeks later, Helen returned to my office and told me that she wanted to work with me on the topic of remorse.

"I was raised in a very traditional way," Helen began. "We were taught not to show any emotions. I was never hugged or kissed by my family. The first time I was hugged was by a white woman. I was about 14 years old, and when she hugged me it scared me to death. When I was 14 they gave a test on the reservation and me and another girl got the highest test scores. We were both sent to Utah to a white family. They were Mormons, and they took in native kids. My friend made the adjustment. She finished high school with them and then went on to the university. I couldn't adjust. They food was weird, the people were strange, and I was so homesick for the reservation that I asked to be sent back. After six months I was sent home. Everyone made fun of me at first because

I talked white and acted white. Eventually, I got accepted. I never finished high school. I got my GED here. I got pregnant at 16 and then that was my life.

"They say I don't get paroled because I don't show remorse, but I don't know how to do that. It reminds me of that time when I was 14. I don't know what they want. I have tried to live a good life on the inside for the past 23 years. I admit I was a troublemaker for the first seven years, but then I gradually came to understand that the trouble was within me not on the outside. Do you think it would show remorse if I wrote a letter to the family saying I was sorry? That every day I pray for that family? If I had it to do again, I would do things so differently. Do you think any of this would help?"

This was a true conundrum. Would the family want to hear from this inmate who was involved in such a horrendous crime? Was Helen truly remorseful, or was she using the letter to the family as a way to try to win her release? If she were truly remorseful, how could she show it when everything in her culture had trained her to deaden all of her emotions to the point where they were no longer accessible to her? If I were related to someone who was the victim of a violent crime, would I want to hear from the perpetrator? How could one ascertain that her apology was sincere? Eventually, I counseled her to write the letter, but not send it. She could, of course, do whatever she wanted, but she agreed that she would write the letter and then we would discuss what she wanted to convey both to the family and to the parole board.

On my drive home that evening, I had many theological and legal questions running around in my head. I could now see that being a chaplain was indeed different than being a psychology intern. The women could have chosen to go to a psychologist, but they chose to come to a chaplain. Some of this choice is cultural, in that they were more familiar with religious people than with psychologists, but part of their choice was an expectation of what would happen in the sessions. There is an authority contained in the role of chaplain that I needed to accept and step into. Hearing the truth of an inmate's life story, or hearing the truth about their crime, was something I was expected to do.

I still felt unsure about the role of repentance in forgiveness. Was there a universal forgiveness that came to all of us? Could we be forgiven if we did not ask for forgiveness? Was remorse a necessary step on the path of redemption? What is the role of remorse in our justice system? Webster defines remorse as having a "tortured sense of guilt." Why does the legal system care if people show remorse? The justice system isn't a church that works with confession, guilt, redemption, and forgiveness. Why would the legal system find it necessary for the criminal to display a "tortured sense of guilt"? Why not just ask the criminal to sign a contract that says they will never again commit a criminal act? Is there some perverse way that our judicial system wants the criminal to act like a cowering, guilty dog, so that people on the outside can feel better and superior? Helen could never learn to do this. She was stoic in her appearance, and a very proud woman. She was denied parole each time she came up for review. She told me she fully expected to die within the prison system.

Because Helen's crime was committed on the reservation, which is federal property, her crime and punishment were under the federal judicial system, whose sentencing was longer than state systems for the same crime. Even though she was not the perpetrator of the crime, she ended up with a longer sentence than the person who actually committed the murder. Where is the justice in this situation? Did Helen deserve to live and die in prison for her part in the crime? I don't know. I do know there were people who did worse crimes who were sentenced to less time. Our justice system is not blind. Class, race, jurisdiction, and gender are lenses through which our judicial system is administered, and if you are non-white and poor, the system does not work in your favor, regardless of your crime.

That May, I graduated with a Master of Divinity. I made the decision to continue on in seminary, and was accepted into a Doctorate of Ministry (D. Min.), specializing in pastoral counseling. Even though my work at the prison was difficult, it felt crucial to me, and I wanted to get better at the work I did. The D. Min. program required two years of counseling classes, and then a dissertation project that I foolishly thought I could complete in one year.

I returned to the institution after taking a three-month summer break. During that time Amber had been released, and Helen had been denied parole one more time. Fall always felt like the season of redemption to me. The hot, sticky, windless days of summer had passed, and the foggy, dreary days of winter were held at bay. It was a time for spiritual reflection, knowing that winter was just around the corner. I reentered the institution with a renewed sense of commitment and hope.

Chapter Ten

CON ARTISTS

Nobody should ever feel embarrassed if they've been victimized by a con artist.—Bradley Skolnik, state Board of Law Examiners, Indiana.

Perky is not ordinarily a word that comes to mind when I am dealing with the women in prison, but perky was definitely the word that came bouncing into my office and asked me what I did. She was about 5'4" 105 pounds with shiny, curly auburn hair, deep brown eyes, a toothpaste perfect smile and even white teeth. She had a sweet and deferential demeanor as she greeted me.

"Hello Chaplain, may I come in?"

She was very polite. I ushered her into the office, closed the door and asked how I could be of help.

"Well, I'm not sure, what do you do here?"

I explained to her about pastoral counseling and spiritual direction.

"Oh, spiritual direction sounds good," she instantly replied.

"Well, actually, I don't do spiritual direction, but I can make an appointment with one of the Catholic chaplains."

She switched gears so fast on me that I didn't even notice she had done it.

"Oh, I was brought up as a Christian Scientist, but I am studying to become Catholic, so I guess I'm not really a full-fledged Catholic who could do spiritual direction. Do you have time to talk to me now? By the way, my name is Maggie." At the time, I did not notice that she was one of the few women who introduced herself using her first name.

"Certainly," I responded. "How's it going for you?"

"You know," she said with a big smile, "it really isn't so bad here. Have you ever been to an overnight spa?"

Pause. The correct answer here would have been, "Why do you ask?" I was new and unskilled, and replied without thinking.

"Yes, I have."

She beamed that seductive smile at me and I felt special. I felt as if I were the most important person in her universe and that she and I had just crossed over into being the best friends ever.

"I think this place is just like a spa," she said.

Really," was all I was able to get out as her answer quickly brought me back to reality.

"Absolutely. I get up early, walk around the track, play tennis, work out in the gym, take some classes at night. You just have to know how to program yourself."

"Well, I suppose."

"Of course, there are a few drawbacks, like the food is terrible, but then you can always buy good food from some of the Mexican women. They are so talented with what they can make and cook in the microwave. The enchiladas are delicious, but they are a little fattening," she said and a small frown flitted over her beautifully composed face.

"But then again, I am working out all of the time, and I have lost weight here, so no worries."

We sat in silence for a moment, and then she continued, "I believe we should fake it 'til we make it.' Don't you?"

"Well, yes. I do think that's a good approach."

"It's always been my philosophy. I hear from the other women that you are someone who can be counted on. I really appreciate that someone like you shows up here and does this work. It is very commendable."

"Thank you," I said, again feeling a little back on my heels. I realized that she was not only in control of the conversation, but I was feeling really good with myself and happy to be with her. I tried to put the focus back on her.

"Did you have a religious upbringing?" I asked her.

Again, the little frown passed briefly across her face. This time I saw her change gears.

"My parents were Christian Scientists, but they didn't bring me up that way. I think my mother was the one who had the biggest influence on me. She told me to always be positive, be dedicated, and loyal and that nothing was more important than your word."

I learned later that she was in prison for running clinics that falsely promoted a cure for cancer using medicinal plants from Mexico. The clinics were very successful as evidenced by the fact she had more than a one million dollar restitution bill to pay once she was out of prison. When she said she believed in faking it until she made it, she was really saying to me that she was faking it all of the time.

One of the things I learned about Maggie was that she was an acting major at a university in southern California, and she had always loved the stage. It seemed as if the whole world was a stage for her and we were all her audience.

I became part of Maggie's programming, and she showed up religiously once a week as promised. She was always charming, happy, positive, and filled with flattery. For the first time in my life, I experienced the down side of charm and optimism. It was as if I were forced to eat nothing but homemade chocolate walnut brownies all day. The first session was delicious, but eventually I felt sickened when I saw her name on my call-out sheet. She was always the same. A sunny disposition, perfectly pressed uniform, perfectly curled hair, perfectly polished teeth and a sweet disposition that would gently question me about my life. When she asked me the name of my church, I asked, "Why would you want to know?"

She responded, "Because you are so great, I would love to experience the congregation in your church community." Right.

I was pretty much at my wit's end in working with her. Unity is a church of positive thinking, but I found in this woman that there is a dangerous seductive side to positive thinking when the goal is to con others. After a few sessions, I found her cheerfulness exhausting and her personal questions set me on edge. I talked to my supervisor, Dr. Ruth Ann Clark, about her.

"Ruth Ann, I don't know what to do with this woman. I don't feel like I am making any progress with her. I think everything she tells me is BS. I have no idea how to get through to her. Do you think if I got mean, or sharp or insulting that would help?"

Ruth Ann seemed slightly taken aback at this suggestion and suggested I do dream work with her.

"You know Susan, our unconscious is something we can't control. Why don't you ask her to journal her dreams and see where that leads?"

It turned out to be an excellent suggestion. The women at the prison loved dream interpretations. Whenever we would have a group offering a dream workshop, it would be packed. Lori and I did the workshops together. We used the method described by Jeremy Taylor in his book, *Where People Fly and Water Runs Uphill*. Jeremy is an ordained Unitarian Universalist minister and taught several classes at the seminary I attended. He suggests the following steps in dream interpretation. One, all dreams speak a universal language and come to the service of us for the benefit of our health and healing; even the purpose of nightmares or bad dreams is to get our attention. Two, the dreamer is the one who interprets the dream. Our subconscious uses our own personal symbology to communicate. When the dreamer has an "aha" experience, that is evidence of the true meaning of the dream. Three, there is no such thing as only one meaning to a dream. All dreams have multiple meanings and levels. Four, dreams do not come to tell you what you already know. The purpose of the dream is to impart some unknown knowledge or solution to a problem. Jeremy also suggests that we title our dreams. Often dreams come in three parts that can be how we interpreted as problems we have had in the past, how we are solving problems in the present and how we can solve our problems in the future. Helen was very interested in dream interpretation and we spent the rest of our time together with her dreams. The following is a dream that had the most impact on my work with Maggie. Through the interpretation of the dream, I learned things about her that she had never told me in regular sessions.

The dream has three parts. She titled the dream, The Getaway, The Reunion, and The Escape.

The Getaway

I am meeting someone outside and they have a car. I'm in the backseat of this government car and there was only one person in the car, me, and I knew there was supposed to be two. There was no driver. My job was to escort people to China for the government. I had to be very sneaky so as not to arouse suspicion. The driver appeared, and then I told him I needed to go back because I knew something was wrong. When I got back people were glad to see me. I knew this was how it should be.

The Reunion

I'm in an airport and I run into my first boyfriend who is a doctor. I tell him what I'm doing and he was surprised and impressed. He thought I had a cool job.

The Escape

There is a group of people and we all must escape. I am in charge. Everything is orderly. I am calm, alert and in control. The house has no doors but it opens to a large white beach. The carpet is the same color as the beach.

A little boy is there and he wants to spray water on the carpeting. He is playing but I tell him he can't get the carpet dirty. There is a huge fence we have to climb to get away. I know I can climb over it but I don't know about the others. I know if I can get to the ocean I will be safe. I hear my mother's voice tell me there is a gate in the fence, and the gate is open. She pushes on it and walks through.

When we started to do the interpretation of the dream, she told me that the sand reminded her of Pirate's Gold, the video game. The beach was the same beach as in the movie *The Shawshank Redemption* (a favorite movie of all of the women). The government was her enemy. An escort was a female escort who worked for the government. Her association with the ocean was interesting. She said it reminded her of God, nature, and that she was drawn to it even though she was afraid of it. The ocean represented deadly beauty. She loved adventure and hated things that were always the same. She loved the idea of a passageway, of going somewhere, of taking on something new.

Her overall interpretation of her dream was that she sees things differently than others. She realized she didn't take time to think about her options. The first thing she sees, she does it even if there might be an easier way to do something. The dreams eventually led into a more realistic telling of the story of her life. She was raised with a sister who was in a wheel chair. Maggie always wanted to find something that would cure her sister, and she believed that the medicine she found in Mexico would work. She had two children, but she couldn't be with them so she gave them to her mother and sister to raise and thought they would be better off without her. She was a hard worker and picked men who weren't always good for her. Immediately after she was married, she found multiple identifications in her husband's wallet and wondered if he had killed the people whose IDs he had. She was loyal to him because she gave him her word. She had a restaurant in Mexico on the beach. She wanted to go back even though she knew it was dangerous.

As is the case with many inmates, the telling of her life was told with big blocks missing, and some of the events made no sense. Husbands were married and divorced without difficulty. Children were happily given to others. She went to Mexico to find a cure for her sister, and then set up multiple clinics in the United States, making a lot of money. Then, for no reason, she went back to Mexico and bought a restaurant on the beach. She loved the restaurant even though she was held up at gun point several times. Yes she faced down machine guns but she told me, we can't dwell on the negative things. She missed her children but they really were happy where they are. It was unnerving to hear this "everything is great" approach applied to her life.

There was no time during our work that Maggie expressed a sense of responsibility for her life. Since she kept saying that prison was a fun, good place for the time being, there was no opening for her to reflect on her crime that led her to prison. When I brought up her children, she said they were very well off with her family, and they didn't need her at this time in their lives. Her optimism stood her in good stead. She was released while I worked at the institution. She came in to give me a cheerful goodbye and wished me luck in my work.

I dealt with other con artists at the institution and they all had some similarities to Maggie. They were above average in looks, and were focused on an orderly appearance and existence. They exercised regularly and controlled their eating. They would spend hours discussing every calorie they had eaten and how much exercise was needed to make up for their diet. They had extroverted personalities and were always, always, cheerful. Even if they told me something that was sad, they were able to cry with tears that never left their eyes or touched their cheeks. The women con artists that I knew seemed to always be patrolling their surroundings, more than the other inmates. They reminded me of sharks who are always swimming, never asleep and never at rest. They were smart and quick witted. Did they believe their own cons?

My experience was they didn't disbelieve them. The question of Truth, as we understand it, seemed irrelevant to them. They had no judgment on themselves, always searching for the next adventure, the next way to make themselves happy. They didn't appear to me to be mean or cruel, just focused on their own happiness. If something or someone got in their way, that was their problem, and unfortunate but it had nothing to do with them. Prison was good as long as you kept busy, went to the gym and didn't get fat. They were happy. To be that happy in prison takes a unique denial system.

I cannot understate the attractiveness of female con artists. They are experts at gaining the confidence of others. They are good listeners, intelligent, and imaginative. When they turned this charm onto the male staff, many of the men were seduced. One woman told me happily of the game that she played when outside personnel came into the prison to replace items in the vending machine. This woman had a spotless reputation and was granted the unusual privilege of cleaning up the visitor's area that contained the vending machines. She knew the route of each of the service men and on the days that they would come to refill the machines, she made sure she was on duty. If there was a new man that was on the service call, she made sure she had on her push up red lace bra and would unbutton her blouse as she bent over to help the young man fill the machines. His flustered embarrassment delighted her. It was a game she often played, perhaps to balance out the power, and she never got caught, to my knowledge.

The con artists I knew would usually start out telling me a "happy" story of their life, where everything was perfect and in order. Then into this "perfect" story of Americana, there would be a jarring detail, such as going through her husband's wallet and wondering if he were a murderer. In another case, a woman was telling me of her idyllic life in Florida until the Drug Agents burst into her house, and she went for the machine gun under the bed and shot it out with the agents. These discordant details would give me a jolt, but they seemed to have no effect on the women. If their masks slipped, they would easily slide back into role and say something Scarlett O'Hara-ish such as, "Oh, let's not think about that now. Let's think about that tomorrow." They were addicted to the adrenaline rush that came with the criminal life where living was easy, fun and exciting. I never had one con artist express regret for her actions, including abandoning their children, and none of them ever talked about the straight life with anything except disdain.From a theological perspective, the con artists were the most challenging population for my work. Where was God in our interactions? Can God show up in an atmosphere created by artifice and lies? My belief is that I know that God is always with us, but if God is in the relationship how does that work when one person is pretending to be someone else? How did I find the spirit of God within a woman when I couldn't find the woman? I wondered about the role I was playing in these artificial relationships. Why would a con artist come to a prison chaplain to begin with? Maybe I was an easier target than the psychology department.

It is difficult to have a pastoral relationship with someone who has no conscience, and yet they too are God's people, so I felt I had some role to play with them, but I was unsure what. Sometimes they would tell me they were sad, but they mainly were sad about being caught, or making the wrong criminal choice, or the wrong choice about partners. True regret, remorse or guilt was not in evidence. Rationality, defensiveness, and manipulation were always at play. I never saw one of the con artists express anger. I never saw them show frustration or cynicism. They were always calculating some game. It was hard to know the game they were playing, but there was always a game. The psychological term for the con artists would probably be antisocial personality disorder. This disorder is diagnosed by people who don't conform to the law, are deceitful, impulsive, persistent lack of taking responsibility and lack of feeling guilty about wrong doing. Sounds like a good description of the con artists I encountered, but from a theological perspective what is to be done?

It became a red flag for me if I felt immediately charmed by someone. Antisocial personalities were only too easy for me to love. They were entertaining, upbeat and fun, and also very, very dangerous. Perhaps I was drawn to them for the same reasons as they were drawn to crime. With time, I learned to keep my guard up. Eventually I could instinctively parry any personal questions no matter how well meaning or crafted they appeared. Perhaps I was as much a challenge to them as they were to me, or perhaps I was just someone they could pass the time with until their release.

I worried that once I left the prison site, I would lose my natural trust and openness with people. That has not been the case. I am still drawn to people who are entertaining and charming, and I have learned the limitation of that part of one's personality.

Chapter Eleven

OUR MOTHERS, OURSELVES

I would have gone home to my mother, but I wasn't that crazy about her.—Cher

The lanky blonde leaning against the doorframe was very still. When I looked up, I wondered how long she had been standing there watching me. Like the other women in the prison, she was dressed in the standard-issue beige pants and short-sleeved, box-cut top, but she wore them with flair, the short sleeves neatly rolled up above her elbows and the top tucked in. She had on new tennis shoes rather than the prison issued heavy work boots. She had probably been a very pretty woman once, but time had taken a toll on her. Her front teeth were tinged a light brown from, as I later learned, a long-standing heroin addiction. Her blonde-gray hair fell in soft curls around her face and her bangs ended just above her pale, blue eyes. She had on mascara and soft pink lipstick, but other than that, she wore no makeup. Although she always seemed tall to me, she, like my mother, was only 5'4" tall and probably weighed about 110 pounds.

"May I come in?" she asked politely. I nodded at her to sit in the empty chair across from me. There was stillness about her as she sat and examined the room.

"How may I help you?" I asked breaking the silence.

"What do you do here?" she replied with a fake, brittle smile. There was something about her that immediately irritated me. I

157

sat for a minute considering my responses and then answered, "I'm a chaplain intern. How can I help you?"

Her response surprised me.

"I want a Buddha statue that I can lock up at night away from these thieving women," her voice rose slightly in a flash of temper. "These women steal anything that isn't locked down. Having a Buddha for my meditation is my religious right. I want a Buddha and a lock to lock it in a cabinet. We're guaranteed the free exercise of religion by the Bill of Rights. You may not know, but freedom to worship is the only right that prison can't take away from us."

What she said was true. Even in prison, the women had the right to worship as they believed. Why would she assume that I didn't know what was in the First Amendment?

"So you're a Buddhist." I remarked.

"I am a Buddhist. It is very important to me, and I think I should be able to have a Buddha when I meditate. You've got all kinds of Christian symbols here. Right outside you have the picture of the Virgin of Guadalupe, you have crosses on the walls. Why can't I have a Buddha?"

"What's your name?" I asked her, as I took out my pen and paper.

"Miss White, but you can call me Eileen."

"Well, Ms. White, who have you talked to about your request?"

"I talked to all of the chaplains. They say they're going to do it, and then nothing happens. It's not fair. If they don't do something, I am going to file a grievance."

"Ok. Let me see what I can do." I stood up from my chair, a signal for her to leave.

"Well, good luck with that," she said with a half smile.

I closed the door and thought, "I do not want to work with that woman. Something about her irritates me." I later saw Chaplain Becker and told him about my interaction with her. He and I had developed a friendlier more relaxed relationship now that CPE was over.

"I know, she wants a Buddha," he said with a shake of his head. "I have so much paper work on my desk; I just haven't gotten to it yet."

"Is there anything I can do to help? I think it might be a good thing for my standing here if I could make this happen." He agreed, and the Buddha statue showed up several weeks later.

Eileen came by to thank me and asked if she could come in to talk.

"So, I hear you're in seminary. Is that right?"

"Yes, it's a Christian seminary." I could hear the tension in my voice.

"Well, what are you studying there?"

"Mostly subjects relating to Christianity."

"Have you taken a course in Buddhism?"

As luck would have it, I had taken a general course in Buddhism as part of degree fulfillment. I told her I had taken a foundational class in Buddhism. She continued to question me, and I continued to answer with short replies. She thanked me for my time, and told me she would be requesting a call-out to come and have pastoral counseling on a weekly basis.

I walked into Chaplain Becker's office, and noisily closed the door.

"I don't want to deal with Eileen. I am not a Buddhist, and I don't think I should have to talk to her. I have a full schedule, and I really don't have time for her, and I don't know that much about Buddhism, and I am sure that she should talk to someone else."

Chaplain Becker turned from his computer, and for the first time since I had known him, seemed slightly surprised at my outburst.

"Whoa. What's going on with you?" he asked simply.

"I don't know."

"We got Eileen the Buddha statue. She seemed genuinely pleased about that and has been using it in her meditation. I thought you wanted to work with her."

I stood staring at the floor, saying nothing.

"I don't want to work with her. She asks me all kind of questions."

"You don't want to work with her because she asks you questions?"

"I don't want to work with her because she's Buddhist," I responded, and as soon as I said it, I knew it wasn't true.

"Really? Well," he responded rationally, "I'm not a Wiccan, or a Muslim, either, but we work with all faith traditions here in the institution. Is that right?"

"Yes. You're right. I'm sorry. She's just difficult for me."

"Hmmm. She doesn't seem difficult. Every time I see her, she has a book in her hands, and she meditates regularly. I think it would be good for you to work with her."

I wanted to shout "Fine" in my best adolescent tone of voice, but I was 58 years old, and had a modicum of control over myself. Actually, there was much about Buddhist philosophy that appealed to me. Besides my experience at "Buddhist Boot Camp" I had enjoyed my class in Buddhism, and I was very drawn to many of the Buddhist precepts. I knew my problem with her was not that she was a Buddhist. I decided to analyze my reaction to Eileen later.

The next week when I went in to get my call-out sheets, I noticed that Eileen was the first name on my list for the morning. Great way to start, I thought.

Eileen came in with a list of books she thought I should read. After I admitted I hadn't read any of them. She chastised me for my lack of knowledge.

"I don't know what that seminary is teaching you."

"I told you, I only had one class in Buddhism." I felt defensive and inadequate at the same time.

"Right, well there is a lot for you to learn. Once you finish this book list, I can always give you other lists if you are interested." I said nothing.

Eileen continued with her questions.

"I would like to have you explain to me the difference between pastoral counseling and regular therapy."

This was a question everyone wanted answered, including me. I tried to respond as best as I could.

"The methods of counseling between secular therapy and pastoral counseling are the same. There are some pastoral counselors who are trained as Jungian analysts, there are those that are trained as client centered therapists, and then there are those who are trained as eclectic therapists who change technique based upon the situation.

"Some of the differences are that when you go to a pastoral counselor you are working with a person who acknowledges that they are a person of faith. As a pastoral counselor, I am interested not only in your relationship with others, and introspection about yourself, but I am also interested in your relationship with God. Additionally, pastoral counselors are generally not held accountable to the state for their licensing and supervision but to their own church community."

"What church community are you responsible to?" she asked.

"Unity."

"Is that the same as Unitarian?"

"No. It's different."

"Are you going to a Unity seminary?"

"No. I'm going to a Presbyterian seminary."

"Oh, well, all you Christians are the same to me. See you next week."

After she left, I glanced at the reading list she gave me and tore it up. I can't believe this inmate gave me a reading list.

The next week, Eileen came in and asked me if I had ever heard of her. I was unsure what she was asking me.

"I'm sure you've heard of me. I was known as the elegant bank robber," she said proudly.

"You were a bank robber?" I asked, wondering where the Buddhist part fit in.

"Yes. I'm sure you saw me on CNN."

"No, I didn't see you."

"Well, maybe you saw me on Fox."

"No, I have never heard of you before."

"Oh well," she said as she slumped back in her chair, clearly disappointed. "I just thought maybe you might have seen me on TV. A lot of people did. I'll bring you in my FBI flyer the next time I come."

She continued to tell me inconsequential things about her week, and after fifty minutes she got up and left. After that meeting, I requested an hour with Chaplain Becker to try to understand my reaction to Eileen.

"So why do you think this woman is so irritating to you?" he seemed genuinely perplexed by my annoyance with this one inmate.

"Well, first of all, how can she be a Buddhist and a bank robber? Doesn't that seem a little contradictory to you?"

"Does it seem that way to you?" he asked.

I sat there trying to figure out the true source of my irritation, but I couldn't think about anything except how annoying she was.

Chaplain Becker continued, "Does she remind you of anyone? Was there anyone in your life that was irritating to you in this manner?"

Silence. Then, bingo. There she was again. My mother. Ugh. Not only did Eileen act like my mother, with her disapproval of whatever I was doing, she seemed like my mother with her lanky body and pale blue eyes. My mother's favorite form of communication was either ridiculing our mistakes or grilling us on historical facts, in hopes that we would make a mistake. When was the Battle of Hastings and why was it important? Diane would ignore the questions, but Sarah and I would spend our time searching the set of the Encyclopedia Britannica to find these historical facts. I wanted to win our mother's approval, and Sarah wanted to outsmart her. One of my mother's favorite comments was, "What is that school teaching you anyway?" Eileen's questions brought that childhood sense of inadequacy back to me when she questioned me about Buddhism. I glanced up at Chaplain Becker. He could tell I had made some type of connection.

"I guess this means that I should continue my work with Eileen."

Chaplain Becker smiled, and responded that it would be a good thing to discuss with my supervisor and grapple with the effects of countertransference.

I continued to work weekly with Eileen. One day, Eileen came in and told me she was ready to talk about her childhood. This was unusual, as every time I had asked her questions, she brushed them aside and gave me a report about the latest book she had read. Eileen was smart, and a voracious reader, and so there were many books she reviewed with me. Although she came every week, always on time, our conversations were more intellectual discourses than counseling. It had been very difficult for me to get her to talk about her inner life.

"I hate people who blame things on their childhood," she began, "I think it's the ultimate cop out. I'm not blaming my childhood, but lately I've begun to think again that part of my humanity is missing."

"What do you mean by that?" I asked.

"I don't know. A big chunk of my heart got betrayed and harmed. I don't try to dissect it; I just accept it. It's just sometimes I don't act like I wish I would. Like last night, I was really mean to this young woman and made certain that she knew I thought she was a stupid bitch. Care and compassion are the first things that go when I'm under stress. It isn't just me though; meanness is in the system here. That's not an excuse. That's just a fact. Some dumb broad goes off her meds last night and keeps all of us awake screaming. Finally, I yelled out, 'Shut the fuck up.' God, sometimes I can't take it. Then I feel bad." She stopped and I thought again of the many ways that being imprisoned ate away at the women, and how much I would hate to be cooped up day at night with twelve hundred women.

"You asked me before about my first memory. The very first thing I remember is my mother picking me up from my crib and how happy I was to see her. I think that was the first, but the memory that has always stuck with me occurred with I was maybe 5 years old. I was in the car, sitting in the backseat of our old beige Chrysler. Really ugly car. Mom left me in the car so she could pick up her paycheck at the mill. It was raining really hard. I remember the big puddles and the rain hitting against the water. She locked me in and told me to stay put. It was thundering and lightening, and I got scared. It was dark, but it wasn't night. It was just one of those dark rainy days we often have in Oregon. I remember staring at the door of the car, hoping she would come back soon. But the lightening seemed to be getting closer and closer to the car. I got worried about it hitting the car, and there I was locked in," she paused for a minute. "Kind of like here." Eileen laughed as she realized my reaction to her memory.

"Don't look like that, Chaplain Pohl. My mom came back. I was happy to see her. So what does that mean?"

"I don't know," I said. "I think we should talk about it later. It's the beginning of your story."

"Yeah, some story."

When she left, I began to think about her expression, "part of my humanity" is missing. Eileen had used it several times, and each time I asked her to say more about what that meant to her, but she wouldn't engage with me. I think that it was her code for having no empathy. Later, she told me that she didn't really feel guilty about robbing the bank; she felt guilty because she had broken one of her Buddhist vows. This lack of empathy made me think of my mother. When Diane was diagnosed with cancer, my mother's first reaction was why did she have to have a daughter who had cancer? I remember at the time thinking, what about Diane? Why is this always about you? How could Eileen be working on compassion, and yet have no empathy for the people in the bank? How could my mother consider herself a Christian and yet behave as she did? How do parts of our humanity go missing? What causes this? Are the parts retrievable?

At our next session, Eileen came in wanting to continue her talk about her childhood.

"My parents were both of Irish descent, which I guess helps explain my whole damn addiction thing. My dad took off when I was two years old. For me he was a non-entity. My mom said that he was an alcoholic, and no good. After he left, we never saw the bastard again. My mom remarried to my stepdad, but I never felt any closer to him than to my real dad. I don't think he ever liked me either.

"When I was between six years old, my stepfather's parents babysat. Don't remember much about them. They had a little farm out of town and they watched me during the day when my mom and stepdad were at work. I remember playing with the animals. I've always loved animals. I had compassion for them, as if I remembered how it was being one. Anyway, the father of my stepfather got arrested for sexually abusing one of the girls in the neighborhood, and they decided it must have happened to me too. I have no memory of it. What I do remember is going to the doctor's office and being asked a bunch of really embarrassing questions, and then being examined. It was awful. We never talked about it after that. In my family, if you didn't talk about it, it didn't exist. But after that, it seemed like my mom was really distant with me. I hate to say this, but I think my mom was afraid of me. I know she was when I got older. I know I've always been a big disappointment to her. I started out as tainted goods and guess I ended up that way.

"In junior high, I began screwing my science teacher. That was a lot more fun than I thought it would be. I started using and selling drugs when I was thirteen. Heroin was, and has always been, my drug of choice. I continued using for the next 24 years. First time I got clean I was 37 years old."

After Eileen left, I began to think about all of the women that I had met at the institution who had been sexually molested before the age of ten. I think this type of molestation takes a chunk out of the hearts and souls of the women and they lose parts of their humanity. Most of the women that I met, who had been sexually abused, had no respect for any type of authority, including their own. Thinking about all of this, I began to feel really discouraged once again. Where to begin with these problems? How can you hold people accountable when they have "part of their humanity missing?" I understood the rage behind Eileen's outbursts, rage about a sexual violation that could never be talked about. She also felt rage against a memory she could never access, and against a mother who felt emotionally inaccessible. All of this rage brought me to think of my own mother and her rage. I never knew if my mother had been sexually abused or not. I know the family story was that her father had to leave the state because he was caught having sexual relations with a niece. I always wondered about him and my mother.

At the prison, the women often congregated first by race and then by crime. The radicals, what few there were of them, stuck together; the drug dealers hung out together; and the bank robbers hung out together. According to Eileen, the bank robbers were at the top of the social heap in prison because they had done what was essentially a man's crime. They held thieves and dealers in contempt for their lack of expertise in committing their crimes. Before I knew it, Eileen had referred me to every bank robber at the prison. Trisha showed up one day and told me that Eileen had referred her. I was not surprised when she told me she was in for bank robbery. She told me she wanted to "work on her shit" so she could get to visit her daughter again when she was released.

Trisha, who stood about 5'4" tall, was 36 years old with green eyes, blondish brown hair and of Norwegian ancestry. She was an attractive young woman, although her nose had been flattened in a fight and her skin was tough and weathered from the time she spent homeless on the streets. Since coming to the institution, she had been lifting weights, teaching a spinning class, and running daily on the track. She told me that other inmates had approached her about how to get into good physical shape and how to change their eating habits. She told me that Dr. P, who thought everyone in prison was overweight, told her that she was the "perfect" weight. She told me that when she got depressed, she remembered what Dr. P told her and remembered that at one point she was perfect about something.Around our third or fourth session, Trisha came in to the office and was very restless. She had missed our last session, and it was the first time she missed.

"Trisha, how are you doing?" I begin.

"I was upset about our last session. Things were stirred up about my dad, and I didn't want to get into it. I loved my dad and he loved me. There was nothing creepy about it. Why does everybody assume there was something bad? I don't want to talk about that," she said, almost screaming at me.

In the previous session, Trisha had told me about walking down a long canyon with her father. She said that she was so proud of herself because she had made it down the canyon and back up, and that her father had rewarded her with an ice cream cone once they got back. Her outburst surprised me.

"Okay. What do you want to talk about?"

"The addict part of me is driving me crazy." I used "parts" as a vocabulary for Trisha to differentiate her personality, and to see that not all of her was an addict.

"What's the addict part doing?"

"It's making me exercise like a maniac, and controlling every morsel of food I eat. I have some underground anger about missing last week. I didn't want to miss, but I didn't want the 'light of God' people to see me because I will hurt them and disappoint them."

"By 'light of God' people do you mean me? Do you think you are going to hurt and disappoint me?"

"I don't know. I know I don't want to. I am starting to trust you, but I'm scared. What if you recommend me to be put on drug or suicide watch once you see I'm not perfect and I'm broken?"

"Are you feeling suicidal?" I asked the question now without flinching.

"No. I can't sort all of this out. I've never been with a religious person like this before.

"Eileen says I need to talk to you about something, but I don't think it's important to my life now, you know what I mean. Things that happened a long time ago, why bring them up? Why can't we just talk about the future?"

"Is that what you want to talk about?"

"I don't know. I guess. You know I robbed banks to support my heroin habit. I think as long as I don't use again, I won't rob banks again, and I won't get in trouble again."

We sat in silence.

"Okay, so the thing is I'm worried about my daughter. I'm not really worried. I'm just thinking about her. You know what I mean. Well, you know when I was using, it was a big mess. So when my daughter was nine months old, I gave her to my dad and my step-mom to raise her. I couldn't give her to my mom 'cause my mom is a whack job. She's still partying, and I can't imagine her raising my daughter. Last week, I get a postcard from my dad that says he wants to formally adopt my daughter. She will be five this year and will be almost seven when I get out. I think maybe he's afraid I'll take my daughter from him. I don't want to take my daughter; I just want to be able to see her. When I was using, they wouldn't let me near her. I can understand that. I got to think about this for awhile. I don't really want to get into it. I gotta focus on staying straight and staying off the streets. When I lived on the streets, it was hell. I remember my dude and me were working, valet parking some cars in San Francisco, and someone left their cell phone in the car. Can you image, how stupid? Anyway, I called home and tried to talk to my daughter, but you know, she knows I'm her mom, but little kids don't talk much. My dad didn't really want to talk to me either. Then two years later, I get this postcard asking about adoption. I haven't talked to them since that time on the cell phone two years ago. I don't know what to do. I got to think this through." Trisha left and never came back.

Weeks later, Eileen brought up the topic of Trisha in one of her sessions.

"I guess Trisha's bailed on you," she started.

"Well, she hasn't been here in a couple of weeks."

"Yeah. I know you told me we can't talk about her, but we can talk about her if it affects me, right?"

I nodded.

"I'm really mad at Trisha." Eileen stopped speaking. I said nothing.

"You want to know why I'm mad at her?"

"Why are you mad at her?"

"Trisha told me when she was eight years old her dad began sexually molesting her, and it went on until she married her idiot husband, the one who got her hooked on drugs. I told her she should tell you about this, but she didn't want to. Now that creepy father of hers wants to adopt her daughter, who oh by the way, will be the same fucking age that Trisha was when he started up with her, and Trisha just signed the gd papers. How could she have done that to her little girl? She knows what a mess that crap causes. How the hell could she have done that?"

We sat in silence for several minutes.

"Sometimes we let each other down." I said. "We try, but sometimes we just don't make it."

"I know. She was giving me some b.s. about how her father has changed now that he has this new wife. It's all a bunch of crap and she knows it. Anyway, it's not my life. Not your life. Screw it."

I later went to talk to Chaplain Becker. After he listened to the story, he said he would call child protective services in the state where Trisha's family lived. He said, without a complaint, or an incident to report, it was unlikely anything could be done. I told him that Trisha would not sign a complaint, since she had just signed the formal adoption papers. I told him that she would deny any of it ever happened.

"I'll do what I can, Chaplain Pohl. We can at least give protective services a heads up."

I later contacted the psychology department to see if they thought Trisha would be a good candidate for their incest group. So many of the inmates had been incest victims that the psychology department held an ongoing group therapy class for them, with a backlog to get in. Trisha refused to attend because she said nothing inappropriate ever happened. She said Eileen made the whole thing up because Eileen wanted attention. Trisha never spoke to Eileen or me again.

Once again, I felt depressed and impotent in the face of the cycle of abuse—crime and abuse. When I talked with my therapist later, we discussed my urge to save the world. I said not the world, just a few of these women. Maybe it harkened back to me being a kid and wanting my gold stars, or, more realistically, I had my own fantasy of being rescued. I used to dream that my mother was actually my adopted mother, and my real mother would one day come and find me and take me away. I was never rescued and neither would they be. I thought about mothers and daughters and the struggles we all have to be independent and yet stay in relationship. How could Trisha have made the decision she did? It seemed like the best option to her. Her mind was closed to the fact that she had perhaps put her daughter in a situation that would harm her.

Eileen was one of only a handful of women I saw that came every time. Many of the other women were hit or miss. One time, they would say they couldn't come because it was movie night, and they had popcorn. Another time they had class. I would bring up the subject of making and keeping commitments, but it never seemed to get much traction. Some inmates always showed up and some were sporadic.

The next session after we talked about Trisha, Eileen was giving me a book review of her latest favorite book, *The Time Traveller's Wife*, when she said, "You want to know the worst thing about being locked up? The first thing is the strip search. It's dehumanizing. They do it, even when they don't have to. A lot of the women here won't have visits because of the strip search. They make you strip, spreading your cheeks, and then cough. It's perverse. You have no control over anything here. Then they presume that you lie one hundred percent of the time. No matter what the circumstances, we are the ones who are always lying, and we are always wrong. Do you know what it's like to live in a system like this with a bunch of crazy lunatics? And I'm only talking about the guards." Eileen started to laugh as she continued.

"Although I have to tell you, Chaplain, that federal prison is better than the state prisons in Oregon. Did I ever tell you I escaped from one of those? One day, I just couldn't take it anymore. It was minimum security. I had a job where I could walk outside without supervision. So one day I just kept walking. I only had to pull another six months before I was out. The escape was a boneheaded move on my part, but the women all thought I was great. I got picked up the next day. I had no ID, no clothes, and no money. Idiot! Got an additional year added on for that stupid mistake. Now, here I am, 57 years old and in a federal prison. If I don't make it this time, I won't survive another period of lockup."

"How do you plan to stay out?"

"Not doing heroin. God it sounds so simple. If I do heroin, I rob banks; if I don't do heroin, I don't rob banks. You don't know what it's like. People make fun of heroin addicts because they say all we do is nod off and sleep, but we aren't sleeping. We are in another state. Imagine it's like you've been cold all of your life and someone comes in and wraps a warm blanket around you. That blanket, my friend, is heroin. It's the only thing that has never lied to me. "H" delivers always, every time, exactly as expected. Booze doesn't do that; men don't do that; only heroin has never disappointed me. It is my old reliable friend. The only problem is it's damn expensive. Unless you're a rock star, you got to do something like rob banks to pay for your habit. Let me tell you something, if you see an addict and they've made it clean and sober for one day, you say, good job. None of you have any idea."

"How did you get off heroin when you were 37? You said you did heroin for 24 years and then you went straight. How did that happen?"

"I didn't tell you that? I got pregnant. Shocked the shit out of me. I always thought I couldn't because of my prolonged drug use. So I kicked it. Horrible withdrawal. I actually really liked being pregnant. I had a job. I figured I could support myself and the baby. I found out it was a boy. I miscarried at eight months. I was hysterical. I wanted to see the body. They wouldn't let me. I don't know what they did with him. This bitch of a nurse told me I lost him because of my habit. I told her I wanted a funeral for the baby, they said they didn't do that. Case closed."

"I'm so sorry, Eileen." For the first time since I'd known her, Eileen got tears in her eyes.

"It was a long time ago chaplain. A lot of water under the bridge since then."

"Do want to talk about it the next time? Do you want to do a service?"

"NO. I don't believe in any of that. Hand me a tissue. I gotta put my game face on before I go out of here. Can't show up on the compound acting like a weak sister. The only place it is safe to cry is here and in the shower."

Eileen dried her eyes and left.

As I was leaving for the day, I walked out into the lobby and noticed a woman sitting in the chair in the hall by herself.

"Do you want to come in and talk?" I stopped and asked her.

"I don't have an appointment." She answered in a meek tone of voice.

"Are you free now?" I asked her. She said yes, so we went back to the office. I unlocked the door and let her in.

"What's your name?"

"My name is Maria," she said and I smiled. I think ninety percent of the women in prison are named Maria.

"Well, Maria, how can I help you?"

"I don't know Chaplain. I hope you don't think I'm crazy, but I feel the pain and suffering of all of the women here, and it's wearing me out."

"What do you mean you feel all of the pain and suffering of others? How do you know it isn't your pain?"

"I don't know. I just can tell it's other people's and not mine. It's always been this way for me. I just feel the pain of people and there is so much in this place; it's unbearable."

Maria had a very quiet, understated, pretty demeanor. She had no tattoos and was very well spoken, with just a hint of an accent.

"Is this pain you feel the hardest thing for you in being here?"

"No," she said and started to cry. "The hardest thing is to be away from my children. I have a boy and a girl, five and seven, on the outside. We're from L.A., so they can't get up here to see me very often. I just can't believe my life has turned into this. I was a heroin addict. That's true, and my husband was a dealer. That's also true. But I never sold one drug. Not one, never in my life. The feds knew that. I was incarcerated under the conspiracy laws."

"What do you mean by that?" I asked.

"We didn't know it but the feds had our phones tapped because of my husband. One day, a call came in and I passed on the message to my husband. I got seven years, the same as my husband. Seven years for taking a call. I had no prior arrest record. Seven years, and my babies taken away from me." She started sobbing again. I consoled her, and she asked me to pray with her, which I did. The next day, I asked Chaplain Becker about the conspiracy laws and if what Maria told me could be true.

"What she says is true. It is one of the tragedies of the situation for these women. The conspiracy laws were originally enacted to give the feds a weapon against crime syndicates. The law says that if you conspire with someone to do something, that if carrying it out would break the law, it is a conspiracy and you can be arrested for it. For women, this has been a devastating law. Women who live off the proceeds from illegal drugs, whether they take drugs or not, or whether they sell the drugs or not, they can still be arrested and booked and convicted on conspiracy charges. We have a woman here from Mexico. She had a two-year-old son. The husband was violent, so she crossed the border illegally to live with her sister in San Diego. She didn't know that her sister's husband was a dealer. She never took drugs, never did drugs. They arrested the dealer, the wife, and the sister, and put her child in foster care. It makes no sense, but this is the way it is now."

"How long has this been going on?"

"The law was passed in 1988 as part of the Anti-Drug Law. That coupled with minimum sentencing can result in the woman I just described getting five years for living with her brother-in-law who was a drug dealer. The logic is that the women are living off ill-gotten gains from drugs. It could have been worse, she could have gotten seven years."

"But what she did isn't at all the same as doing the crime. What was she supposed to do?"

"The law says she should have turned her brother-in-law into the law."

"That's ridiculous."

Chaplain Becker shrugged his shoulder. He seemed tired, and so was I.

The time working at the prison was beginning to take a toll. I was never sure exactly what I should be doing. I believed it was best for me to show up and try my best, but was that good enough? I knew I had perfectionist tendencies, and I certainly wasn't perfect at this work. Working with women who were in such fragile situations alarmed me. My supervising professor told me that the one documented element in the efficacy of any type of counseling was the bond that was built between the client and counselor. I knew I was trying to build a bond with them. I did genuinely care about each and every one of them. I still believed that hearing someone's story was a sacred responsibility and I knew that these women didn't have many people who could genuinely listen to them. I prayed for courage, resilience, and the ability to forgive myself and others.

I returned to the prison the day after meeting Maria with a renewed focus and determination to do better. I started spending more time in meditation. I continued to say my prayers as I went in and wash my hands and say my prayers as I left.

One day, a new woman named Lisa came in. She didn't know anything about me, but just happened to walk into the office hoping she would find someone to talk to. She said she loved God and she loved Jesus, and I told her to come in and sit down and talk. She told me that she and her mother came out of Ohio and were hooked up with the mob. Something happened, and they were relocated to outside of Las Vegas. She said that her mother ran a well-known whorehouse on the outskirts of that city. She said that her life was pretty normal in Ohio when she was little. Her grandmother had been really nice to her and they had baked chocolate chip cookies together. She said her life was never normal again after she left Ohio.

"What do you mean it was never again normal?" I asked her.

"My mom embarrassed me a lot when I was growing up."

"How did she embarrass you?"

"One time, I finally talked a friend into having a sleepover at my house. Usually, the parents would find out who my mom was, and they wouldn't let the kids come over to stay with me. I told my mom this was really important to me that I had a friend come over, and she said she knew and she would be on her best behavior. We picked up my friend at school and Mom said she had to stop and get gas. We asked if we could go inside and get Slurpees, and she said sure. She was always good about stuff like that. My mom was driving a bright red Cadillac convertible. Everybody in town knew her car. So we go in to get the Slurpees, and she goes out to pump gas. Then I guess the car behind her gets too close to her, or I don't know what happened, but she starts screaming at this guy to "back the F up" and he isn't doing anything, and starts mouthing off to my mom. That's the one thing you can't do is mouth off to my mom. I could have told him that. He keeps yelling at her. Then she gets real quiet. Opens the back of her car, takes a rifle out and shoots the hood of the guy's car. Can you imagine how embarrassing? They called her 'Mad Dog Lola.' I never got another friend to stay over after that."

"What happened to your mother after that?"

"She never got arrested or anything. She paid everybody off, so she could pretty much do what she wanted. If my mom were alive, I would never be in here.

"All I have ever wanted is a little farm with a lemon tree and a pony. I used to tell her that, but she thought I was nuts. She told me with my build, I could make a lot of money. I did for a while, hanging out at the Four Seasons, better group of people there. I don't like people that much. I wanted to be myself. My mom thought I was really weird. For one thing, I loved country music. No one in Vegas liked that kind of music. She said she thinks I liked country because of my dad. She would never tell me who my dad was. It's blank on my birth certificate. I figured out though that it was probably Elvis. They all said he liked that kind of music. I kind of look like him, don't you think? Not that it would ever do me any good if he was my dad, especially now that he is dead and all."

Lisa later told me she had been sexually abused starting when she was ten years old, after they moved to Las Vegas. Her mother worked nights, and she was left alone with her mother's live in boyfriend. She told her mother that that boyfriend was molesting her, but her mother didn't believe her. She hated the boyfriend and the things he did to her. She said she hadn't even started to menstruate yet, and didn't really know what was going on.

She and I continued our sessions for several more weeks. One of the things I sometimes did with the women was ask them to draw their family in four stages of their life, (for example one to ten, eleven to thirteen, fourteen to twenty-two, twenty-three to present.) On another piece of paper, I asked them to draw their image of God for the same four stages. I had them use colors for the drawings. After they did the drawings, I told them I wanted to see if anyone in their family carried the color of God. Generally, there was one family member that the woman would associate with God, and I tried to get them to talk about that person and what was special with them. As I talked to them about the God-like characteristic they saw in their family member, I told them that they, too, had that characteristic.

When Lisa was drawing her pictures of God, there was a yellow box in the quadrant from ten to sixteen. I asked her how the yellow box represented God, and she said it was Jesus lying in a coffin while she was being abused. She said, "You can't blame Jesus for me being abused if he was in the coffin." It was easier for her to put Jesus in a coffin than to express her anger about the situation.

Many of the women I saw were released during the time I was there, and this was always a day of celebration. As they got ready to go out into the "real" world, they carefully dispersed their treasured belongings to the remaining inmates. Friends did their hair, they received real clothes from the outside, and then they were on their way. Usually, a line waited to watch them as they left. We waved, hoping never to see one another again. Many of the women left in fear that they would not be able to withstand the temptations of life outside, and many left with fear of people from their former lives. I learned that the undocumented women were sent back to their country of origin. Eighty percent of the female inmates at Federal Correctional Institution Dublin at that time were from Mexico, and most were undocumented workers. Once they completed their sentence, they were put on a bus, given $200, and bused into Tijuana. I heard terrible stories about the women being raped and robbed of their money once they got to Mexico. When I asked about this practice, the officers told me that the arrival time of the bus was supposed to be kept secret, but once the women crossed the U.S. border, it was no longer the government's responsibility. I understood this, but still...

That summer I took another break. After my return, Eileen came in and gave me a secret hug. She wanted to know what I had done, where I had been. I gave her a vague, abbreviated version, and then turned the conversation to her. She told me she had been back in touch with the Buddhist Rinpoche she had worked with. He had invited her to stay at the monastery once she was released. His vote of confidence not only lifted her spirits but also motivated her to continue with our work together and try to make more progress in understanding herself.

I asked her about her periods of sobriety and what had caused her to relapse each time. She told me again about getting pregnant, kicking heroin, and then losing the baby. She said she did heroin the day she was released from the hospital. She talked to me again about being a bad daughter. How her mother was always disappointed in her, and she could never be what her mother wanted her to be. Betrayal and trust were her constant dance partners. She would trust people, and they would betray her. People would trust her, and she would betray them. It was an endless dance.

She told me when she was in first grade, her mother kept her home from school for an entire year because of some unknown disease. She had to stay in bed, and all she could do was read books. An ongoing regimen of antibiotics exposed her to the magic of drugs at an early age. When I asked if this were before or after the doctor examined her for signs of sexual abuse, she appeared shocked, said she didn't know, and kept talking. When she went back to school following her illness, she didn't fit in.

Bigger than the other kids and better read, she was picked on. She remembered feeling lonely and unable to connect to anyone, and couldn't recall having any friends.

Eileen believed she had been living in the Buddhist plane of the hungry ghosts who were always hungry, always hunting, always hunting for the next thing to satisfy them but nothing ever did. In a land of food and water, the hungry ghosts die of hunger and thirst. I asked her how she could change this story and she said she didn't know. If this story were her karma, how could she change? I suggested she write to her Rinpoche and ask him about this.

As we began pulling back more of the onion layers of her memories, she seemed to muster the courage to continue to dig and try to understand. We spent no more time on book reviews; each appointment became a time of intensive self-examination. She seemed to think her time was limited, and indeed it was. She told me that she kicked heroin again in her late forties.

"What motivated you to do it?"

"God! This is a terrible memory. My lover at the time was Ray. We had decided we were going to try to get straight and kick it together. We found a street clinic. We went through the really hard work together. I really thought we both would make it. I got a good job. We got a little apartment together. We were living like normal people. One night Ray came home and I could tell he was high. I started screaming at him. He denied that he was using, but I knew. Of course I knew and he knew that I knew. I kept screaming at him, telling him how he let me down, how he let himself down. I was crying, he was crying. He walked out the door and I followed him. I just couldn't help myself. I was telling him how much I hated him, what a weakling he was—all of the things that I thought about myself. All the way down the stairs I kept screaming at him, on and on. He got to his car. It was parked on the street under a street lamp. I didn't want him to go. I didn't want him to drive. Still I showed him no compassion. I was in such a rage. He said to me,

"Just a minute Eileen; I have something for you." I was sure he was going to give me drugs. I was screaming at him I didn't want any of his gd drugs. He reached into the back seat and took something out. I couldn't really tell what he had, but I remember suddenly feeling cold. The next thing I knew he put a gun to his head and blew his head off. Right in front of me. That son of a bitch. He blew his head off right in front of me. I had skull and brains all over me. Standing by that car, him on the pavement, once again, cleaning up a mess. I was tempted to pick up the gun and do myself, but I just couldn't do it. Maybe I was too scared. I don't know. I had to call the gd cops. That was a treat all right. Right away they see I got a record, but there was no way they could pin this on me. What a son of a bitch. What a son of a bitch."

We sat together in silence for what seemed like hours, but was probably just a few minutes.

"Here's the irony, Chaplain: after that I got straight and stayed that way for 18 years. It might have only been a veneer of respectability, but I had a veneer for 18 years. I faked it for 18 years after that no good son of a bitch blew his head off."

Eileen left and I thought about all of the women that I had met here. The ones who were difficult to talk with, the ones who just wanted to sit with me and cry in a safe place. There were women who asked if they could come in and listen to soft music while they drew. The office was a sanctuary for the broken, and I included myself in that group. There was woman who came in who had never had a prior arrest. Never even had a traffic ticket. One day she decided to take herself off her antidepressants. She went into a manic attack and started robbing banks. She started with her own bank. She never spent one dollar that she stole, she just wanted to do something. When they arrested her, she had four shopping bags of cash in her dining room. She was fifty-eight years old. The judge didn't know what to do with her. She returned all of the cash, but because of minimum sentencing, she was sentenced to three years in federal prison. Was that justice?

One of the exercises we used to do in theological reflection group was to complete the following: There is no such thing as justice there is only_____." Depending on my mood or experience of the day, my answer to this would either be practical or hopeless. The day of Eileen's visit, I finally decided on my answer. There is no such thing as justice; there is only God's grace.

Eileen came back the next week, and announced she would be released in the next few months. The reference from her Rinpoche, who promised to vouch for her, had secured her a spot at a halfway house near the monastery. She felt overwhelmed by his kindness and terrified of messing up again. We had worked together for almost four years, and she wanted to complete the work we had begun. She said she wanted to be realistic. Burdened by a $47,000 restitution fine, she had no idea how she would pay it off at the age of 58, making minimum wage.

We started the story again about her relapse.

"For eighteen years you were sober and straight. What led to your last relapse?"

"No excuses. I had a run of really bad luck. I had a really good job in customer service. I was doing AA regularly. I was being really careful. Then three things happened. The first was my stepfather had a heart attack and died. I was never really that close to him, but it really rattled me. He was with us one moment and gone the next. Then my aunt who I lived with was diagnosed with ovarian cancer. She was so depressed, and so was I. The final straw, though, came with Frank, my boyfriend at the time. I was working late, and got off early. I went to his apartment and found him in bed with one of the people from the AA program. I mean, who did he think he was messing with? I went into a rage. I picked up a sledge hammer from the garage, and beat the shit out of his car. Scared the crap out of him. What a dope. Unfortunately, I started back again. I thought I could handle it, but it gets out of hand. Was doing H again, and started robbing banks." As I listened to her story of betrayal and rage, I was taken back, once again to my younger self.

One Saturday morning, I had my ironing all laid out, and I was in a happy mood. I was 11 years old, and I was paid two dollars a week for my chores. It seemed like a fortune. Sarah, my younger sister was outside playing with a friend. My dad was at work, and the house was quiet. As I was ironing one of the pillowcases, I heard screaming that pierced all the way down to the basement. I knew it was my mother and my sister Diane. Diane was 17 at the time, and in constant adolescent battles with my mother. I hesitantly walked up the basement stairs to the kitchen and paused to listen. I realized the screaming came from the top floor where the kids' bedrooms were located. This was really bad. My mother's bedroom was on the main floor and she rarely went upstairs, but when she did, all hell broke loose. Usually, the target of her anger was the mess in our rooms. One day, she took all of our drawers out of dressers, threw them out the second floor window, and said we had to leave them there until Dad came home. Once he got home, Mother said Sarah and I had done it. My father was incredulous and kept asking why we had done such a thing. I kept quiet, but Sarah told Dad mother had done it. He didn't believe her.

I heard my mother screaming, "I wish to God I had never had you shitty ass kids. What the hell is wrong with you that you have all this shit up here?" I heard my mother pick up a dish and throw it down on the wooden floor shattering it into pieces.

"How many times have I told you, don't bring food upstairs. What the hell is wrong with you? Are you deaf? You've got chocolate hidden up here too? You're not going to get rid of those pimples on your face if you come up here and stuff your face with candy. What else do you have hidden up here?"

Suddenly I heard Diane respond.

"You know what? You wish you never had me, well, I wish I never had you as mother. I hate you. Bitch!" I was stupefied. No one had ever back-talked my mother like that. She responded in a steely tone of voice I had never heard before.

"How dare you speak to me like that? Who the hell do you think you are? Who in the hell do you think you are I asked?"

I heard a slap, and then Diane screamed, "Don't you touch me. I hate you. Do you hear me? I hate you." I ran to the bottom of the stairs, not knowing what to do, and saw them wrestling with one another. My mother grabbed both of Diane's arms and threw her backwards down the flight of stairs. Diane crashed down, knocking parts of her arms and legs as they bounced off the wooden steps. She landed at my feet crumpled into a ball. It had all happened so fast. I stared down at Diane and thought she was dead. My mother continued her tirade from the top of the stairs. I was terrified of my mother, but now I felt more afraid that she had actually killed my sister.

"I swear to God, Diane, I brought you into this world, and I can take you out of it. I'll kill you if you ever speak to me like that again. I swear to God, I will. Do you hear me?" my mother raged, gasping for breath at the top of the stairs.

I had never seen anyone thrown down a flight of stairs except in the movies, and then they always were dead. I was sobbing, looking at Diane, who had not gotten up.

"Diane, are you ok? Oh, please say you're okay. Please get up. Please get up," I stooped down and whispered to her, as she lay at the foot of the stairs not moving.

"Diane, can you hear me? Please wake up. Diane, wake up," I sobbed, not knowing what to do. Diane slowly roused herself, and leaning on me, she stood up with her hand at the back of her neck.

"Come to the basement with me, and let Mom calm down." I said as I led her through the kitchen and down the stairs to the basement. She said nothing. I sat with her on the couch and continued to try to make contact.

"Diane, are you ok?" I was crying. "Diane, please talk to me. Are you ok? Diane, can you hear me? I don't know what to do." I reached out to touch her, and she recoiled from me, as if I had shocked her.

"God damn it, Susan. Leave me alone," she finally responded to me. She started to heave with sobs, and I left her. I went out the back door from the basement and sat in our backyard. I secretly thought of tape-recording my mother's violent episodes and playing it in church, but I wasn't exactly sure how to do it or if it would make matters worse. Everything I thought of seemed impossible. I couldn't think of anyone who could help us or stand up to my mother without me getting killed. I sat in the backyard staring at the canal until Sarah came up.

"Hi," she said and sat down. Her blonde pigtails were tied with ribbons, and she played with the ends of them as she sat down next to me and caught her breath.

"What's going on?"

"Mom threw Diane down the stairs." Sarah at first seemed scared, but then she set her jaw and turned to me.

"Is she okay?" "I think so, but if I were you, I would stay away from both of them."

"Okay," she said, and ran back to the neighbor's to play.

That night when my dad came home, no one mentioned anything. My mother was in a happy mood and had fixed a special lemon meringue pie for dessert. I thought of that constant sense of cognitive dissonance and how I had the same feeling here in prison. I looked up, and I realized that Eileen was staring at me. I sensed a yearning in her for something from me, but I was unsure what that was.

"I guess we all try our best, and sometimes our worst self gets the better of us," I answered.

Eileen started to cry and so did I.

Eileen was released a few months later. She wrote me a very moving thank-you note for the work we had done together. One of the last things she asked of me was to please write this book to make sure that women in prison did not remain the forgotten of the forgotten.

"Don't forget us Chaplain."

"I won't," I answered, and I have not. The women are in my heart now and will always be.

With hindsight, it seems evident that my mother was mentally ill, like many of the women in prison, but in the fifties no one talked about mental illness or how to cope with it. Years later, one of my aunts told me that my mother was kept in bed for a year when she was seven years old because she had killed a cat with a broom. The cat had jumped in a pie that was sitting on the windowsill to cool. My mother flew into a rage, started beating the cat and killed it before anyone could stop her. Her parents knew this was not "normal" and the doctor diagnosed her with St. Vitus's dance, which was associated with rheumatic fever. They wanted to believe she had accidentally killed the cat, and this diagnosis seemed like as good a reason as any. I thought about my mother and Eileen both being kept in bed for a year. My mother's behavior initially was worse than Eileen's. Killing an animal is a sign forewarning of dangerous mental instability. My mother killed an animal and Eileen loved animals. Eileen turned to drugs and my mother turned to religion. My mother certainly made the better choice as far as outcome is concerned.

Mothers and daughters keep swimming in and out of my consciousness: Eileen and her mother, me and my mother, Trisha and her mother, Lisa and her mother. This relationship that carries so much expectation can also carry so much pain, disappointment, and betrayal. I believe that it is possible to overcome a mother who is dysfunctional, but it is difficult. I was very lucky; I had other strong women in my life who loved me and nurtured me. Sarah and I came out okay, while Diane really struggled in life. When I think about my mother compared to all of the other mothers I heard about in prison, I began to see her and her rage in another light.

If a woman had a mother who could not protect her, such as Lisa had, what did that do to her self-image, her soul, her very sense of who she is? If one had a mother like Trisha's, who partied and slept with the same men that her daughter slept with, what kind of mother could we expect Trisha to be? If you had a mother like Eileen's, who was there but not accessible emotionally, what does that teach you about your relationships with others as well as your relationship with yourself? The cycle seems unremitting to me. Anger, violence, abuse, addiction, crime are all interwoven and begin at the beginning, with the family, and it reminded me of my own family.

My mother's rage could have landed her in prison had fate gone another way. Diane could have died when my mother threw her down the stairs. My mother also once tried to run over my dad with the car when she thought he was cheating at tennis. If she had killed him, she would certainly have gone to prison. I learned that the women that I met in prison were more than their crimes, and in learning this, I began to accept that my mother was more than her rage. All of these women were people with a history of loving, having fun, struggling, failing, trying to do better, doing worse, and ultimately being human. My mother, like Eileen, was smart, funny, and strong. I had developed true compassion for Eileen in my work with her. How could I have less compassion for my mother? When I realized that I truly loved Eileen, I also realized that I loved my mother as well. We all try so hard, and fall so hard. Skinned knees and all, we get up one time more than we think we can.

I realized that among all of the women I met, and all of the mother/daughter stories I heard, I was the lucky one. I had a father who loved me and was very active in the family. I had an older sister who tried to protect me and a younger sister who could validate my reality. I was blessed with teachers who took an interest in me and other women who loved and valued me. Their support helped to make up for the deficit of parenting from my mother. The gift of faith I had as a child helped me, and the gift of intellect I had as an adult helped me to understand by mother's psychology and see her behavior apart from me. None of the women I met in prison had my good luck of circumstances. My luckiest break of all is that I was never sexually molested. My positive sense of self built as I aged. I had some success in life and, therefore, I knew that I could be successful.

During my time at the prison, my mother died. She was 92 years old. Her goal was to die in the same room she was born in and she accomplished that, with the help of my sister Sarah. At the end of her life, my mother turned into a little girl, hugging her teddy bear. She was nicer than she had ever been to my sister and me. Sarah said it was because she didn't recognize us. I thought maybe the tough painful edges of her raging personality had been dissolved with time, and that she turned into a nicer person. My last visit with my mother, I had a tender sense of love for her that I had never felt before. She was so childish and vulnerable. She died peacefully in her sleep during an afternoon nap.

Once Eileen left the institution, I was finally able to finish my work there and leave. That was the hardest decision I ever made. Since they had no one to take my place, my sense of guilt in abandoning them was enormous. I stopped seeing new inmates, but one of the women I had been seeing had a life sentence, so I could not wait until she was released to release myself. Four years had passed since I'd started my assignment there. As in any counseling relationship, the termination phase was extremely difficult. Some of the women handled this stress by just stopping, and refusing to say goodbye. Others wrote letters to me and handed them to me on my last day. Due to security concerns, I was told that I could not correspond with the inmates once I left. The inmates and I both knew that our goodbyes would be final. I left with sadness for the women but also for myself. My faith had never felt stronger than it was in prison. I felt alive, that my life mattered, that I had made a difference in the world. There is an old hymn that is often sung at funerals called, "It is Well with my Soul" by Horatio Spafford that captures my feelings about my time at the institution.

When peace, like a river, attendeth my way,

When sorrows like sea billows roll;
Whatever my lot, Thou hast taught me to say,
It is well, it is well, with my soul.

I always believed that God was with me in prison, and that I was doing what I was called to do.

I continued on with my Doctor of Ministry work and completed my dissertation project in two years. My subject was using narrative with female inmates as a method of counseling. Through my dissertation process, I questioned the amount of time I had spent at the institution. Why was it really so hard for me to leave? Who was I really there serving? Was I serving God, the women, my ego, or just working through my own imprisonment? Like the women I had counseled, who, due to life circumstances or choice, had put themselves in prison long before the law put walls around them, how many prisons in my own life had I created?

Glen Sherley, a former inmate at Folsom Prison once said, "The worst kind of prison a person can be in is the prison of self—to be in bondage to something or somebody enough that it leaves you desperate, with no peace, no hope."

When I was in my thirties, I used to have a recurring dream that I was locked in a dining room littered with remnants of a bountiful Thanksgiving dinner that had been eaten by a large group. The room was formal, with plates made of bone china and water and wine glasses of Waterford crystal. I knew it was my job to clean up after dinner, and I knew I had to do it alone. I was depressed facing the task. I saw a window at one end of the dining room, but it seemed blocked, and the door out of the room was locked. Sometime during the dream, I would always realize that poison gas was seeping in under the locked door. I would wake up terrified, gasping for air. I dreaded going to sleep at night for fear I would have that dream. At the time, I was getting a master's degree in psychology, and I talked to a psychology professor about the recurring dream. He told me the next time I had the dream, I was to pick up a plate and throw it through the window to break the glass and escape. I was able to do what he told me the next time I had the dream, and I never had the dream again. At the time of this dream, I was wrestling with the implications of divorcing my husband. I knew that my life as a southern lady was not the life that was meant for me. It was the unhappiest time of my adult life. I felt walled in by my marriage, the culture, and my own low expectations of myself.

I believe now that we all create prisons for ourselves of one type or another. Some of us have prisons of past injuries that we replay until we work ourselves into a state of vengeance. Others of us have prisons of responsibility and we build walls of resentment that we have to do everything for everyone. Our beliefs that wall us in are as strong as the prison walls covered in concertina wire. A big difference between a physical prison and a mental one is we can break out of our own prison once we acknowledge it is of our own making. What we think about we bring about. Learning to be free took me decades, but eventually, I flew.

Chapter Twelve

FEAR AND LOVE

One word frees us of all the weight and pain in life. That word is love.—
Sophocles

In November of 2008, I made an appointment to see my doctor. I had been having problems with breakthrough vaginal bleeding. In my forties, I had my ovaries removed as a protection against ovarian cancer, seeing that my sister, my aunt, and my grandmother had all died from the disease. Since having my ovaries removed twenty years earlier, I had been on hormones, both estrogen and progesterone. The breakthrough bleeding was new for me, but when I talked with several of my friends, they said that they had also experienced this, and it turned out to be nothing. I was sure mine was the same. When I went in to see my doctor, she suggested I also have a mammogram, and we scheduled it for the first of December.

As I sat busily writing a report for one of my clients, I received a call from the doctor's office telling me I had a recall for my mammogram. I thought at the time, what a strange verb to use, and I felt annoyed. I presumed they had not taken a good image, and now I had to interrupt my schedule and return because of their lack of competence. I was scheduled for a pap smear, as well, and was told I could do that at the same time as the mammogram recall.

I drove to the hospital without calling anyone, expecting that I would be in and out of my appointments in thirty minutes. I had the pap smear and then headed over to have another building for the mammogram. Once I had the second mammogram though, everything felt different. It was as if I were in a movie that suddenly went into slow motion. They no longer rushed me through the system and then sent on my way. Instead, at each step, I was told there would be another step and another test. With each delay, my irritation morphed into mounting concern. Breast cancer had never been one of my many health worries. As far as I knew, no one in my family had ever had breast cancer. I was sure that if cancer were to strike me it would be ovarian, and so I was still relatively calm as I sat waiting for the ultrasound. At the time, I had no knowledge of the link between ovarian and breast cancer. The female radiologist who did the ultrasound seemed very serious.

"Is it cancer?" I asked her timidly.

"I can't tell you for sure, but whatever it is, it must come out." She answered without establishing eye contact with me. I was not relieved.

When she left, one of the nurses gave me the name of a breast cancer support woman. I knew then that things were not good.

I went home and found a message on my machine that said my pap smear needed a biopsy. I was totally stricken with the news. In my mind these two things merged into one. I was sure that I had cancer throughout my body. I felt paralyzed with fear. Gary came home around two o'clock that afternoon. When he left in the morning everything was fine, now at two o'clock my life had been upended. He took one look at me and knew something was very wrong.

"What's the matter?" he asked.

Instead of answering, I held on to him and fell apart. I never really knew what that expression meant before, but now I was experiencing it. The fear in me totally conquered every part of my being, and I dissolved. It was the worst feeling I have ever had in my life. Gary, trying to understand, stayed silent for a while, and then asked me what had happened since the morning.

A few words about Gary, my husband, my stalwart companion, and the love of my life. He believes in data; I believe in intuition. He thinks thoughts quietly and keeps them to himself. I don't know what I think until the words come out of my mouth and bounce off someone else. I am truly curious about other people; Gary is truly curious about ideas and things. At a dinner party, I think the more the merrier; he thinks two people are a crowd. I have a facility for language; he struggles. I tell stories; he laughs. He cooks; I eat. I'm neurotic; so is he. (Fooled you, didn't I?) We both love Italy, movies, reading, and most of all we have loved every dog who has entered our lives, the current one being Luca. It is enough. We have made it together for 25 years. We are both proud of that.

Most people describe Gary as grounded. He did a past life regression one time, and found out he had been a tree for centuries. My Buddhist teacher told me this was not possible, but then he never met Gary. Gary and I met when I hired him to work for me in the human resources department. He says he still works for me. His family background is similar to mine. His father's family was Catholic and his mother's was Baptist. His father was an alcoholic and had similar anger issues as my mother. We understand each other at the deepest level and also at the most superficial level.

Gary held me that day until my body stopped shuddering. He asked me to tell him exactly what happened, and he brought me back to his world of data and facts.

"I think cancer has taken over every part of my being," I told him.

"But you don't know that. What is it exactly that you know for sure?"

I told him about the mammogram recall and then finished with the recall for my pap smear.

In the middle of my explanation, I received a call that I needed to schedule a biopsy for the breast tumor that was found. I had a fatalistic sense about the biopsy. I knew from the reaction of the first radiologist that I probably had cancer. Gary was more anxious to get the results than I was. I thought as long as I don't know the answer, I could pretend nothing had happened. I waited for over a week for the results, and then I got the call.

"As we suspected," the doctor said over the phone "it's cancer." I didn't fall apart.

I guess there is no good way to break that kind of news to someone. My diagnosis was "ductal carcinoma with lobular features, grade II invasive." The tumor was 1.2 centimeters. I think this time it was easier on me than it was on Gary. He really believed that the results would come back that the tumor was benign. I knew better. I later went for genetic testing, and in spite of the geneticist's and my belief, I did not have the gene for breast cancer or for ovarian cancer. Also, my breakthrough bleeding, that had originally gotten me to make the doctor's appointment, turned out to be nothing and totally unrelated to my breast cancer. All I had to face was early stage breast cancer. It was more than enough for me.

I faced my ultimate fear; death and cancer. I responded by cleaning my closets. It was not a spiritual moment. The thought of someone going through all of my things after I died, horrified me. I started with my clothes closet. Would I waste away and finally fit into clothes that were too small? A morbid thought. I decided to get rid of all the clothes that didn't fit, either too big or too little. I was heartless in my disposal of clothing. Nothing was kept because it held a memory of a former good time. As my ex-boss used to say, when in doubt, throw it out. Out, out, out. I felt better.

The next task I had was to notify my friends and family. Because I was diagnosed in December, we already had Christmas plans to fly back east. I elected to have the surgery as soon as possible, even though they told me I could wait. I believed if I didn't get the cancerous tumor out of me, I would die within the next twenty-four hours. It truly felt this way.

I canceled my Christmas and New Year's plan and started to call people to tell them of my diagnosis. It was more fun to clean the closets. First of all, getting the words out of my mouth, "I have been diagnosed with breast cancer" felt like a new diagnosis every time I said the words. To tell the truth, I never thought about what type of reactions I expected from people. I guess I thought people would be like Gary, strong, steady, and reassuring. Might I say, Gary is one of a kind. I heard every bad response imaginable after delivering my news. The worst was from my sister Sarah, who loves me and I love her dearly. Her response was to tell me all of the people she knew that had died of breast cancer and how horrible this was. Decidedly not helpful. I got really mad at her and told her I didn't want to talk to her again until she could locate three people who had breast cancer who were still alive. She called back the following day with a long list of survivors.

The second worst response was someone who questioned my lack of spirituality in the face of my diagnosis. Ahhhh—therein lies the rub. I did not feel the least bit spiritual. I felt afraid, anxious, nervous, and irritated with those around me. I didn't ask why me, I always thought why not me? I was mainly worried, anxious, and afraid of the future, and the unknown. I felt like throwing up all of the time. They had an opening for surgery on New Year's Eve, but Sarah said she thought the hospital staff might be partying while I was under anesthesia. Not a pretty picture, so I said no to that date. I was hoping for a cancellation on the thirtieth, so I had no choice but to sit and wait, to see if someone cancelled, which they eventually did.

Waiting for surgery to be scheduled was excruciating for me. I realized that self-pity was a giant hole in the middle of the road to falling apart. I have never really felt self-pity before, at least that I recognized. It is an ugly emotion. Once I recognized the self-pity-fall-apart monster, I found it easier to avoid. The bottomless pit of my anxiety was not just about the cancer, but the actual realization that I was going to die one day. The veil of denial was ripped away from me when I received my diagnosis. We all know we are going to die, but the personal realization was shocking. The sadness for myself overwhelmed me. I thought about a life gone. Memories gone. Friends gone. How do we live with such knowledge when it is no longer a parlor game or a Buddhist exercise, but an actual event? How to live when denial no longer covers the truth of my own mortality?

Here's how I faced my fear. First, you have to face it in order to neutralize it. For me, prescription drugs helped, humor helped, walks helped, church helped, friends helped. But the one thing that really helped me was movies. I found that watching a really good movie allowed me to immerse myself in someone else's life, their story, their ability to deny the truth of their own death and keep the monsters at bay. Friends were also very helpful to me at this time. My friend Marjorie assured me that there would come a time when I actually forgot that I had cancer, and she was right. Her husband Doug came up to Oakland from Los Angeles and back in one day, just to let me know he was there and he cared. I had people show up at the hospital to sit with Gary and make sure he didn't freak out...he didn't.

Still, a part of me wanted to bargain with God like I did when my sister was diagnosed, but I knew the futility of that, and I had no chips with which to bargain. I had worked with children with cancer, gone to seminary, worked in a prison, not much more I could promise to do to keep myself safe. December 30, the day of my surgery, finally arrived. While under the anesthetic, I had the sensation of Dad putting his hand on the top of my head. I remember feeling comforted and loved.

I was immediately released from the hospital. All of the news following the surgery was good. The cancer had not gotten into the nodes, and the surgeon believed that she had removed all of the cancerous cells. I had a God dream the first night after my surgery. I dreamed I told God that it was hard to feel spiritual when I was so gd terrorized. He told me to watch my language. Humor continued to lurk under the folds of my fear and depression.

My existential questions returned to me. What am I supposed to do with my life? Am I really a spiritual being having a human experience or am I a human being who can imagine a spiritual life? I decided it was time to make a commitment. Do I hold onto my faith or walk away, but walk away into what? The alternative to faith seems to me to be annihilation, nihilism, and total despair. Doesn't seem like a particularly good path. I decided that I was more afraid that faith is real rather than faith is not. To step out onto the water and be held up is much scarier to me than stepping on the water and sinking. The problem is, even if the surgery did remove all of the cancer, I am still going to die. That is a fact. The veil of illusion that covers this fact still floats around me waiting to cover the terror. Facing this truth about death, and my basic fear of annihilation, is something I must do with as much courage as I can muster.

After my surgery, I had radiation for three weeks, and no chemo. Everybody said how lucky I was. I didn't feel lucky. I felt tired. My emotional life was swinging on a pendulum. Hope/doubt, excitement/boredom, desire/weariness, enthusiasm/apathy. The world was twirling around me. I read that if you are worried, you tend to overvalue negative information. I tried to stay in the center. It was hard. Things to remember when people are ill:

Don't ask, "How are you feeling?" We are supposed to say "fine," but if you aren't feeling fine, you don't want to say so and they don't want to hear it. Another irritating question is "Are you in a lot of pain?" What type of question is that? If I'm in pain, I don't want to talk about it. Okay what are some appropriate questions to ask: "How is it going today?" "What kind of day are you having today?"

Every day for three weeks, I went for radiation treatment, and Gary accompanied me to the radiation center each time. I hated every minute there. The machine was like a monster machine from a sci-fi movie. I was pushed and pulled as if I were a slab of meat. I thought about being dead and how my body could be manipulated like this by a coroner. I tried to think happy thoughts but found it almost impossible. Once the machine's computer setting was correct, the technician scampered out of the room, and I was left alone with the machine. I thought about *Space Odyssey 2001*—Hal and me. Mercifully, the sessions were quick. I left the exam room and walked out to the lobby, and there would be Gary, caring, consistent, controlled. My sweet Gary.

I began reading *Staring at the Sun: Overcoming the Terror of Death* by Irvin D. Yalom.

I know now that it is my ego, which controls the fight or flight response for survival, which causes the terror within me. I believe that we go back to the place we were before we were born. For me, this was a lovely place up in the clouds with God. I read somewhere that if we knew the fear the soul had before it was incarnated, we would never be afraid of death. My death experience at Buddhist Boot Camp showed me the everlasting peace of death, and yet...

Waking up at 3:00 in the morning it sometimes felt that my body had a mind of its own; its own agenda. How can that be? Fear has now receded back into its dark cave like a beast that crawls away in the light of day, but I know that it is there resting, gathering strength. How to embrace this beast rather than fight it? Fear and I have danced together my whole life. I had feared my mother's anger. I had feared I would lose the ones I loved and the ones that loved me. I had been afraid to try new things. I had feared rejection and pain. Ultimately, I had feared death. We have danced together for a lifetime; fear and me. We started with a slow waltz, then we did a quickstep through my youth, and now I had just completed a frenzied dance somewhat like the Tarantella from Naples. I have never lost this partner, but now I can look into fear's eyes and not dissolve. I have survived the biggest fear of all, and I am still standing. Radiation is over. I asked my oncologist if I should take my social security early or when I am fully vested. She looked at me for a few minutes and smiled.

"Do what you were going to do before your diagnosis. I believe now is the time for you to live your life and stop worrying about death. You are not going to die of breast cancer."

Still I had to learn to live with the inevitable knowledge of my own death, as we all do. I don't want to live a life of denial but I don't want fear and death to have the upper hand in the time that I have left. Faith will help sustain me but the power that overcomes my fears and my death terror is love. Love, I realized was my final and fifth stone.

How do I define love? For me it is a feeling that is larger than my own Susan ego wants or needs. I loved Marisa, and could easily put her needs above my own. In the pastoral counseling sessions, I could listen to the inmates and put their needs and sorrows above my own. In that moment, or space where we met one another, I had a sense of deep love with the person I was counseling. I have also had this sense of deep love when I have worked with executives in coaching sessions. In the connection, my own ego, fears, anxieties, and needs disappear. Paul Tillich, another brilliant protestant theologian, defines love as the moving power that brings about the unity of the separated. I know that what I seek from other people is a sense of connection because I believe it is in the connection that love resides. There are certain people that I connect with at multiple points. I love Gary in a breadth and depth that I have not experienced with others. I love my nieces Elizabeth and Nancy as I watch their lives unfold and see them develop. As Tillich says "that moving power of life moves me to unite what has been seen as separate."

The most difficult thing for me has been to put this connection and love into practice with my own being. Because of my upbringing I struggled with a sense of worth and value. I constantly felt a need to prove that my life was worthwhile that I mattered somewhere or somehow. Facing death, I know that I have been my true self and that was enough. I have a moving power to unite the separate parts of myself and in that movement and integration; I have finally experienced self love.

Chapter Thirteen

A LIFE REVISITED

We shall not cease from exploration, and the end of all our exploring will be to arrive where we started and know the place for the first time.—T.S. Elliott

---

I have now come back to the beginning of my spiritual story and of the five stones: faith, courage, kindness, service, and love. I realize they have become an ingrained pattern in how I deal with the world. I no longer experience them as separate entities. They have become, for me, not only the meaning of my life but the way I live my life.

I found out that my faith is like a smooth stone in my heart that is sometimes fogged over by life events, but which remains as present as it was when I was a child. I still hold the striped rock to remind me that my understanding of faith is never complete, and part of that is an accepted mystery that I try to hold gently. I think that some people are born with the gift of faith, just as some people are born with a gift for music or mathematics. Some people have no sense of faith, just as it is hard for some people to be introspective, or solve geometry problems. No matter what one's inclination, I believe that any belief in the sense of the common good can be nurtured and developed. I strengthen my faith in many ways now. Sometimes it is strengthened by attending church service, sometimes by listening to religious music, sometimes by journaling my sense of gratitude, other times by quiet walks in the woods or at the beach.

For me, faith is trusting in a power larger than myself. People often say to me, "I don't believe in God." I ask them to describe who they think God is, and when they do I say, "I don't believe in that God either." I believe in a God that is more of a force than a presence. For me, God is an energy that pushes me to be generous, to do a loving thing, to be connected. My trust in this God inclines me to think of the greater good rather than the "Susan good." My faith allows me to affirm the positive in my life and to acquiesce when things don't go according to my plan, knowing that there is a larger plan at work in the universe. I have faith that there is order to the universe and that there is more to our life than the material world that we can see.

Facing cancer showed me that it is possible to have courage and fall apart at the same time. My courage might not have been evident to me in the moment of my terror, but it was there, just as my faith has always been with me. I try to remind myself that being afraid and being courageous can coexist in one body. In my coaching practice, I tell people that my life is grounded in two principles: tell the truth and be kind. Kindness has come easily to me, telling the truth has been a struggle; but I have practiced it, and each time I have the courage to tell a difficult truth it makes the next time easier. It is easy for me to be kind to people that I love and who think and believe as I do. To be kind to people who do not have my values is a continuing life challenge.

Being of service to others has become one of the most rewarding experiences of my life. I am grateful for the advantages I have had. I believe that we are called to care for one another whether we are strangers or good friends. From service, I learned that I got more out of the experience than what I gave. I believe that we are all connected, and when we practice acts that are for the common good we not only make a contribution to society but we strengthen our own character and in doing so we strengthen the bond that holds us all together.

Love has given me the ability to put my own anxieties aside and to focus on a connection with the other. It is deeper than acceptance and more active than kindness. We are told to love God and love each other. How does one learn to love, love? I believe it comes in dropping our defenses. We stop telling the bad stories about ourselves and others. If we truly love, we are moved by the suffering that comes to us all, whether it is caused by illness, death or imprisonment. To move forward in the world with love takes concentration and an observant mind. This is very hard to do when we are frenzied and busy. I have learned to calm myself down and be more present in my life in order to both give and receive love. It is still a work that is ongoing.

I think the most important lesson I learned in discovering and living by my five stones is that I had to go out in the world and experience things in order to find my purpose in life. Going to church with my grandma, going to Buddhist Boot Camp, working with Marisa, going to seminary, and, finally, working at a federal prison, all of these experiences have enriched my life with texture and color. It is important to know that all along the way, I was afraid. I felt inadequate. I felt out of place, unsure of how to fit in, how to make a contribution, how to add value. In Silicon Valley before the bust, we talked a lot about giving back. In order to give back, I needed to take risks, and get out of my own old patterns of beliefs and behaviors. At least that was true for me. I wish you the best in your own personal search for meaning and purpose in your life. Don't give up. It is never too late or too early to think about these big questions. We are all connected. What we do for the least of us, we do for all of us.

And theodicy? What is my belief now? I believe that much of what we see as evil is mental illness. On the other hand, I also believe that we can become separated from our better selves. We become selfish, obsessed with our own material well-being, and we forget that we are all part of the same human race. We lose our sense of humanity when we lose our sense of generosity. We feel hurt by others, we nurse our wounds, and then we retaliate. For most people, including me, turning the other cheek is almost unattainable in the moment. But we can go back and revisit the ones we hurt and that hurt us and metaphorically turn the other cheek. We can stop the cycle of you hurt me and now I will hurt you. We can clean up some of our messes.

There is an old Cherokee legend about a grandfather and his grandson. The grandfather tells the young boy that there are two wolves fighting inside every person. One wolf is evil, angry, greedy, and has self-pity, false pride, and an inflated ego. The other wolf is good and has joy, peace, love, hope, humility, and kindness within him. The young man is silent for a while, and then looks at his grandfather and asks, "But grandfather, which wolf will win?" The grandfather looks at the young boy and slowly answers, "The one you feed, my son. The one you feed." May you all feed your good wolf.

As for me, I only know that for today, I will embrace my five stones: faith, courage, kindness, service, and love. For today, I will be at peace with myself. I will focus on my belief that God is with me, and I will not be abandoned. That belief will carry me through the uncertain times ahead.

First I would like to acknowledge my professors, Dr. Archie Smith Jr., Dr. Sandra Brown, Reverend Hans Hoch, and Dr. Ruth Ann Clark for their help in my religious formation. They taught me to ask the hard questions and be patient in my search for answers that had depth and meaning. I have eternal gratitude for my dear friend Reverend Lori Eickmann who experienced life at the Correctional Institute with me and helped me laugh at the absurdity of many of our circumstances. I would also like to thank my pastor, Reverend Dianna McDaniels who kept my spirit nourished during very difficult times.

A gracious bow to the Buddhist Writing Club made up of Jenny Kern and Sue Moon. They were instrumental in the conception and fruition of this book. Not only did they accompany me through the writing but also through the four years as a chaplain. They were always encouraging, supportive and loving with me and I am eternally grateful.

Next, I need to thank all of my readers who patiently read drafts of this manuscript. Gina Blus, Marjorie Brent, Michael Bryman, Dorothee Bryman, Adelle DiGiorgio, Lori Eickmann, Erin Meadows, Lorraine Reafsnyder, Michael Solder, and Donna Toomey. A very special thank you goes to Dr. Kent Britnall who originally told me that I needed to write this book so that others could share in my experience. I would never have gone down this path without his counsel. Thank you also to Vicki Gibbs, who as my editor kept encouraging me, and Pam Brown, who as the graphic designer, took me across the finish line. A special thank you goes to my sister, Sarah Sharpe who held my feet to the fire in telling the truth about the home where we grew up. She has always shared my reality and my love

Ultimately my thanks go to my husband, Gary, for his support, love and laughter as he and I have experienced the best of times and the worst of times. He has read every single work I have ever written, often multiple times. His encouragement sustained me. He will drag me kicking and screaming into a happy life in Italy.

About the Author

Susan Pohl is an executive management consultant whose clients include Kaiser Permanente and Stanford University. She has a Master of Divinity from Pacific School of Religion in Berkeley, California, and a Doctor of Ministry from San Francisco Theological Seminary in San Anselmo, California. She currently works out of her home office in Oakland, California, and divides her time between her consulting work and her new home in Umbertide, Italy. She is accompanied in her life by the love of her life, her husband Gary, and her newest love, Mr. Luca.

Susan can be reached through her website:
http://www.susandpohl.com

1. Describe a time when you were afraid. Has your experience of fear changed over your life time?
2. Do you believe every life has a purpose, if so what is yours?
3. Do you believe the women in prison are fundamentally different or fundamentally the same as you? How so?
4. Describe a time when you felt imprisoned. What kept you in that prison and what enabled you to get out?
5. Do you believe everyone has a spiritual journey? If so, describe your journey as if it were a road trip. What type of highway have you been on? What type of stops have you made along the way?
6. In our culture, how is grief handled?
7. Have you ever been afraid to do something and then did it anyway? What was that like for you?
8. What is your belief about evil?
9. If you were to simplify your life down to 5 things, what would those five things be?
10. What in this story could you relate to and what was difficult to relate to?

1. Has there been a period in your life when you turned away from your relationship with God? If so, what brought you back?
2. What is your definition of evil?
3. What is your personal belief about evil and an all powerful God?
4. Have you ever had a paranormal experience? What is your belief about the author's vision of her sister? What is your theology around this?
5. What is your experience with meditation? Do you believe it is part of your faith tradition?
6. What is your belief about the Virgin Mary? What is it based on?
7. What is your belief about Divine guidance and free will?
8. Is confession and repentance necessary for forgiveness? Why or why not?
9. How do you believe we receive grace?
10. What role did dreams play in the author's faith journey? What role have dreams played in your life?
11. Describe what service means to you? What are some examples of service?
12. People speak of the healing power of love, what does that mean to you?

5 7
1 9
9 9

Made in the USA
Lexington, KY
30 March 2014